Let's Do Launch

A Hollywood Agent Dishes on
How to Make Your Business and
Career Take Off

Harry Abrams

Founder and Former Chairman/CEO,
Abrams Artists Agency

with Rod Thorn

Brick Tower Press
Habent Sua Fata Libelli

Brick Tower Press
Manhanset House
Shelter Island Hts., New York 11965-0342
Tel: 212-427-7139
bricktower@aol.com • www.BrickTowerPress.com
All rights reserved under the International and Pan-American Copyright
Conventions. No part of this publication may be reproduced, stored in a retrieval
system, or transmitted in any form or by any means, electronic, or otherwise, without
the prior written permission of the copyright holder.
The Brick Tower Press colophon is a registered trademark of
J. T. Colby & Company, Inc.

Library of Congress Cataloging-in-Publication Data
Abrams, Harry.
Thorn, Rod.
Let's Do Launch
p. cm.
      1. Biography & Autobiography—Entertainment & Performing Arts.
      2. Performing Arts—Acting & Auditioning.
      3. Business & Economics—Industries—Media & Communications.
      4. United States—Nonfiction
      Nonfiction, I. Title.
  ISBN: 978-1-899694-12-9, Hardcover 978-1-899694-13-6, Trade Paper

Copyright © 2023 by Harry Abrams

October 2023

Let's Do Launch

*A Hollywood Agent Dishes on
How to Make Your Business and
Career Take Off*

Harry Abrams

Founder and Former Chairman/CEO,
Abrams Artists Agency

with Rod Thorn

To the entire creative community, whose talent and passion has enriched my life and the world around us in countless ways. It has been an honor and a joy to have played a small part in assisting in the development and advancement of the creative expression.

—Harry Abrams

Dedication

This book is dedicated to my wife Gay. Her unwavering support and perspective on life and family has been my anchor for almost 40 years.

And to my children, Tony, Jonathan, Nicolas, Zach, Emily and Maddy; your presence in my life has been the truest representation of my success—you are my legacy!

List of Photographs

Table of Contents

Introduction

The sun'll come out tomorrow.
Bet your bottom dollar that tomorrow there'll be sun...

—Charles Strouse and Martin Charnin
From *Annie*

On a bitterly cold February day in New York City, 1979, I sat in a temporary office with a telephone, a list of names and phone numbers, a pencil and yellow legal pad, and tried to resurrect my life.

I was divorced from my first wife, who was in Los Angeles with our three children. I was in a second marriage, and other than having a son together, it was not going that well. I was in gut-wrenching psychotherapy. And two weeks prior, in an epic betrayal that made front-page news in the entertainment industry, Noel Rubaloff, my friend and trusted business partner, the man who had been my mentor when I was just getting started in the mailroom at MCA, had forced me out of Abrams-Rubaloff & Associates, the talent agency we co-founded in Hollywood 15 years earlier.

Now, in this non-descript New York office, I was starting from scratch. I called myself H.A. Artists Agency, but I had no artists and no agency. I had been working the phone for days with no luck. As a salesman, I was used to rejection. But I knew the people I was calling, and their cold shoulders made me feel like an outcast. If I didn't get through to somebody, or have one of my calls returned, I was going to explode.

1

I stared at my call sheet, and then at the phone for a few minutes more. Finally, I snapped my briefcase shut and got up to leave. With my hand on the doorknob, the phone rang.

I lunged for the phone, then took a breath to calm down. "H.A. Artists Agency, this is Harry Abrams."

"Hey, Harry! This is Bill Haber from CAA."

CAA was the Creative Artists Agency, which was formed in 1975 by the talent agents Bill Haber, Mike Rosenfeld, Ron Meyer, Rowland Perkins, and Michael Ovitz when they left William Morris in the middle of the night and opened their own shop a few blocks away in Los Angeles. They were growing fast and would one day be the most powerful agency in the world. But I didn't know that then.

I squinted at the phone. I hadn't called Bill. How did he get my number?

"Harry?" Bill said.

"Yeah, Bill," I said. "What can I do for you?"

"Well, here's the thing. My partners and I saw the news of your breakup with Noel Rubaloff in Daily Variety and the Hollywood Reporter. . ."

This is it, I thought. He's calling to pick over my remains.

"You saw that," I said.

"Tough stuff, Harry. I'm sorry to hear about it."

"Thanks, Bill. I'll be fine."

"I know you will." Bill said. "That's why I called. We were thinking, my partners and I, would you consider helping CAA get into the commercial business by opening and running an office for us in New York?"

"You mean come to work for you?" I said.

"No, no. More than that," Bill said. "We would want you to join CAA as the sixth member of our senior leadership team."

I sat back down. This was not at all what I expected.

"Well, I'll have to think about that. I just left one such guy after fifteen years. What am I going to do with five!?" I joked.

In the minutes that followed, Bill came on strong, telling me about CAA's plans, their successes, and how driven to succeed they were. In only two years they were already well-known for being ruthless and cunning, and for their take-no-prisoners approach to business. They were signing talent left and right, packaging them with writers and producers and directors, and bending the studios to their will. They were making a fortune. And I stood to make one, too.

As Bill was speaking, the voices of my life's teachers – bosses, teachers, parents, aunts and uncles – kept whispering to me, trying to get my attention. The more insistent they got the more Bill's voice diminished.

That's when it hit me. The voices of my teachers were clear. And what they said to me changed the course of not just my work, but my life. Their advice led me to discover and represent tremendous talent, pioneer new ways of doing business, and have my work recognized throughout the entertainment industry. More importantly, their guidance has made me a better husband, and father, and friend.

What I realized that day is what this book is all about.

The day Bill Haber called I was frustrated, fearful, and furious. How, I wondered, after working so hard, sacrificing so much, and having such success, had it all blown up? How was I going to make my way in the world now?

Anyone with big dreams and ambition is going to face adversity, uncertainty, and injustices. In the entertainment industry that includes loads of self-doubt and huge egos, often in the same day. It has been said so frequently and in so many ways it almost seems cliché to bring it up. Getting knocked down doesn't matter. Getting back up does. Unless you are solid in your beliefs, know who you are, and have a strong foundation you will not be able to weather the inevitable misfortunes life throws at you. Especially in Hollywood, where life is a constant torrent of breakups, breakdowns, and breakthroughs. It can make you wonder why so many people try to break into the business. Perhaps we should take a fresh look at what "making it in Hollywood" really means, given how daunting the task is.

The labor unions, SAG-AFTRA, which brought together the Screen Actors Guild (SAG) and the American Federation of Television and Radio Artists (AFTRA), represents actors, announcers, broadcast journalists, dancers, dancers, DJs, news writers, news editors, program hosts, puppeteers, recording artists, singers, stunt performers, voiceover artists and other media professionals, has approximately 160,000 members. The other major labor union in the entertainment industry, Actors Equity Association, which represents American actors and stage managers in the theatre, has about 44,000 members. Combined, that's 204,000 people who are fortunate enough to have gained entry into these exclusive professional unions.

However, getting into these unions, while a good career milestone, does not equal success.

According to the Bureau of Labor Statistics (BLS) employment (as of June 2016) for actors is so irregular that the agency can only calculate hourly rates for the profession and not the customary annual income. There are 52,620 working actors in the United States, and their median hourly wage is $29.14. The lowest-paid 10 percent make $9.39 hourly, and the highest-paid 10 percent earn over $100 hourly. Those working in the motion picture and video industries make a mean hourly wage of $50.88. Independent actors made a lower average wage at $44.46 per hour. On Broadway, where stages represent the pinnacle of the theater actor's profession, the minimum salary for an actor varied between $236 and $684 a week as of June 2016.

To increase the odds even further, consider diversity. A USC study found out of 11,000 speaking parts in 2014's movies and TV shows, only one-third were female, 28 percent were minorities, and two percent were identified as LGBTQ+ individuals. So even if you do make it, if you don't represent Hollywood's standard, you will still have a hard time finding work. What's more, there is a short window in your life where you can become famous, especially if you're a woman. This is because of the value Hollywood puts on beauty and youth.

With all the challenges facing performing artists, what's it like for the talent agents who represent them?

According to the BLS, there are currently about 13,000 agents and business managers of artists, performers, and athletes. The median hourly wage for a talent agent is $35.45, and their average salary is $49,000. An entry-level talent agent with less than one-year experience can expect to earn an average total compensation (including tips, bonus, and overtime pay) of $37,340.

But there's more to the story. The average yearly compensation for someone in the mailroom of a talent agency, which is how I and most agents got our starts, is about $32,000. When you factor in the approximate $2,200/month cost of a tiny one-bedroom apartment in Los Angeles, whether you're an actor, agent, or mailroom clerk, it is hard to make ends meet when you're just beginning your career in the entertainment industry.

If we pull back a little further, we can understand the anxiety and uncertainty with which today's broader workforce is struggling.

As I write this, about seven months after the inauguration of a new President, a survey by *NBC News/The Wall Street Journal*, found that about 80 percent of voters now believe the United States is spiraling out of control. As consequential as this election was, the usual political debates, campaign events and policy fights have faded into the background for voters battered by a public health crisis, struggling through an economic recession and boiling over with fury over racial inequities. With more than 40 million people unemployed, more than 650,000 killed by COVID-19, and millions protesting racial injustice in the streets, Americans see their personal concerns and political choices through a stark existential lens—lamenting the past, anxious about the present, and scared of the future.

As someone who grew up modestly, in the shadow of the Great Depression, this is exactly what I was feeling when Bill Haber called and asked me to join CAA.

After I hung up the phone, I went back to my apartment and re-examined everything I'd experienced in my life and career—the actors, agents and casting directors with whom I'd worked, the financial gains I'd made, and all the people who had passed in and out of my life as I pursued success. It turned out we were all suffering from a fatal flaw in how we did things. I didn't know who among those people had special insight into the path forward, but I knew I wasn't one of them.

Since that day in that miserable little office, over the course of my career, I've helped famous and not-so-famous artists book hundreds of millions of dollars of work. In the process, I've made a good living for myself, my family, and the agents with whom I've worked. I've had experiences I never would have thought possible. And it's all based on an insight I had when I answered that call from Bill Haber.

In this book I will offer this simple but often overlooked insight that will transform how you work and how you live.

If you ask average citizens what success looks like in Hollywood, you'll hear common themes.

Actors and actresses are rich, liberal, entitled, vain, spoiled, selfish, rude, demanding, philandering, partying, publicity hounds who are surrounded by an army of fawning hangers-on and enablers, and become successful by knowing someone in the industry or sleeping their way to the top.

Same with producers, directors and screenwriters. Although the writers, if they've been thought of at all, will have decidedly more lowbrow tastes.

And talent agents, oh boy. They're rich, flashy, ruthless, unscrupulous, brash, competitive, power hungry, greedy, vindictive, disloyal, dishonest, heartless, conniving, sleaze ball men and women who drive red sports cars, wear expensive bespoke suits, dine at exclusive restaurants, live in several mansions, smoke big cigars, vacation in exotic locales, and also become successful by knowing someone in the industry or sleeping their way to the top.

Finally, probably the most cutting description of an agent comes from someone who was *in* the entertainment industry, the old-time radio host and comedian, Fred Allen: "An agent's heart would fit in a flea's navel and there would still be room left over for two aspirin and an acorn."

How many people in Hollywood start out thinking they want to be everything I just described? How many people ruminate on how badly they want to be rich, egocentric jerks while they alienate their friends and family? I'd say most do not. But there is way too much of this attitude for my liking.

Remember how I said when I got that call from Bill Haber, I began to realize something about success? How I remembered what the people who had given me advice said about making my way in the world? What was their solution? Was it "by any means necessary, extract as much money out of people as you can, regardless of the consequences?"

No. That was not their solution. If I can pick one word it would be "integrity." And by integrity, I mean having a firm and incorruptible adherence to a code of moral and artistic values.

When architects and engineers and builders say a building has "structural integrity" they are saying it is constructed in such a way that it will withstand the years of pressure put on it from weather and time and just supporting its own weight.

That's what I mean from a human perspective.

I knew who I was and what I wanted. I knew my clients and what they wanted. I'd done the hard work of preparing for this moment. I just needed to be myself. And what I was. . .was an agent. Not just any agent, but *my* kind of agent.

The talent I represented didn't care what kind of car I drove or house I lived in or wristwatch I wore. They cared about getting more and better work. Work that was in line with how they saw themselves and what they wanted to do. And in that moment, I didn't care about getting rich. I cared about helping my clients.

After I hung up with Bill, I went back and thought about what to do next. I decided I would take my time and do my due diligence. I'd fly out to Los Angeles and spend some time with CAA's partners. Listen to what they had to say. Get a feel for the people and for the place. This decision was a big one, and I wanted to get it right.

The simple truth was my vision of success in life was not about how much money my clients made for *me*, but how well I served *them*. By serve, I mean getting them more and better work as they define it. And by clients, I mean not only the talent I represented, but also the people who hired them. To me, nobody wins unless everybody wins.

In practice, this means that instead of telling talent how amazing *you* are, you demonstrate by your actions how amazing *they* are. To do that, you help them do more and better work that benefits everyone.

I learned this early in my career when I was part of a very unusual situation that occurred at the Democratic National Convention in Los Angeles in 1960. Having climbed out of MCA's mailroom, I was working in the commercial advertising division. One day, a brand representative from Lipton Tea's advertising agency (Sullivan, Stauffer, Colwell, and Bayles) asked me if I had a celebrity who could be their television spokesperson live at the convention. They would provide the sixty seconds of advertising copy and the performer would deliver the message live when they cut to the commercial. I came up with one of our clients, the late Eddie Albert, and proposed him to Lipton. He was a well-known actor (Green Acres), but he'd never done anything as cold and cruel and crass as television commercials. In those days classically trained actors didn't do such a thing, so he said no at first. But, I reasoned, the money was terribly attractive, and the commercials would only air this one time during the convention.

I was able to persuade Eddie to accept the job, so I negotiated the deal, which involved Eddie being paid half of the money up-front and the other half at the end. The first night, he delivered a couple of commercials during the three-hour telecast. I went home feeling pretty good about things. But later that night Eddie called me and said, "Get me outta this, I hate it!" It was a real dilemma since a good amount of money had exchanged hands, he was already on the air, and they had three or four more nights for the convention to be telecast. I was in a

Eddie Albert

pickle. If I tried to get Eddie to keep his commitment, he'd be pissed, and MCA might lose a client! If I pulled him out, I'd piss off the Lipton people! What the hell was I going to do!?

I didn't sleep much that night, and early the next morning I got a call from Lipton's advertising agency, Sullivan, Stauffer, Colwell & Bayles. Before I could speak, they said they were very unhappy with Eddie's performance and didn't want him to continue. I couldn't believe my ears!

Feigning outrage, I said, "What do you mean you're unhappy with his performance!? He's already gone on camera in front of the whole country. If millions of television viewers know that you fired him it will be terrible for his career. You can't do this, it's ridiculous!" They told me I had to figure out some way to get it done. I got off the phone and thought about it. We represented a lot of well-known on-camera commercial spokespersons during those years, one of which was George Fenneman, who had been the original announcer on the Groucho Marx show "You Bet Your Life." I thought I'd offer George. Mind you, George had no idea this was happening.

I got back to the ad agency later that morning and said, "I'll tell you what, you're going to have to pay Mister Albert the rest of the money. In addition, you're going to have to hire another of our clients, George Fenneman." To my utter shock, they agreed to everything.

I hung up the phone, called Eddie, and said, "I was able to get you out of the Lipton deal, plus you're going to get paid the other half of the money right away." He was glad to be out of the commitment with Lipton, and he was thrilled that he'd be getting the rest of the money while doing nothing to earn it. He called me Harry Houdini. And I didn't even have to tell him Lipton didn't want to continue with him.

As for George Fenneman, Lipton loved what he did at the convention so much they hired him to do all of their television commercials for the next several years. This wasn't just a win. Not even a win-win. This was a six-way win—Eddie Albert, George Fenneman, Lipton Tea, the ad agency, MCA, and me.

Thus, I learned another lesson: people don't care about the absence of your solution. They care about the problems and pain they face in their lives and what you can do to help them.

I learned this early on, and it helped me build a strong career. The more I practiced it the more successful my clients became. And the more successful my clients were the more successful I was. If you put your clients first and focus on solving their problems, you will be well on your way to transforming the way you work.

Over the course of this book, I will show you what you must do to find your success in life. To ensure that you see how universally applicable the concepts in this book ultimately are, each chapter will feature both stories about how I approached my own work as well as stories around how I scaled that success for my clients.

The book will be organized in two parts: Building the Foundation, and Launching Your Career. The framework I'll describe works whether you're an actor or actress, a talent agent, or in some other line of work.

In Part 1: The Foundation, we'll begin by identifying your true calling and assessing your strengths. This will help you take stock of where you are in relation to what you'll learn in the rest of the book. Then, we'll go through a process that will help you take what you've explored so far and chart a course for where you want to go.

In Part 2: The Launch, we'll look at the principles, practices and attitudes that will go into your journey. Over a series of chapters, using examples from my own life, we'll cover topics such as knowing the value of a dollar, developing an entrepreneurial mindset, taking a step back to go forward, humility and hunger, immersion in the arts, negotiating, branding and publicity, diversity and inclusion, ethical decision-making, managing conflict, resilience and the art of the comeback, the work-life balance conundrum, and doing good while doing well. The progression of these topics will help you gradually build more and more knowledge and insight so you can put these methods into practice.

In our current always-on, always-connected world, there are a lot of people shouting "look at me and the amazing things I can do" on social media without much to back it up. And really, no one cares about superficial posturing. Your clients and customers, whomever they may be, want to know that you can solve their problem or alleviate their pain, not your own.

Even though there is a lot of noise to cut through as you move forward with this work, if you follow this framework, you will transform how you see success.

Part One: The Foundation

Chapter 1: Who Are You?

Work is what you do for others, liebchen.
Art is what you do for yourself.

—Stephen Sondheim
From *Sunday in the Park with George*

Like many men, my life was forever changed in the delivery room of a hospital. In my case, it was Kaiser Foundation Hospital on Sunset Boulevard in Los Angeles.

It's 1954, and in those days, the only man in a hospital delivery room is the doctor. But I want to see that magical moment when life begins, and the world is full of possibilities. Will it be a boy or a girl? A doctor? Lawyer? Basketball player? It's thrilling to think of.

I plead with the doctor, "Let me come in and watch the birth process. I won't say anything. You can put me off in a corner." He waves me away, but I pester him until he says yes.

"All right," he says. "Go and get yourself scrubbed up, put on a gown and a mask and come on in. Don't make any noise. Just stay off to the corner." I do as I'm told.

The surgery room, with bright lights and instruments and machines buzzing and several nurses bustling about is exciting.

It's also dangerous. The baby is coming fast so there's not even time for an epidural if one was available. There's a combination of wailing and shouting, calm commands and gentle encouragement. The lights seem brighter. The walls, whiter. The activity, more intense.

Despite the pushing and the coaxing and the urgency it seems there's not enough room for the baby to come out.

The doctor calls for the scalpel so he can do an episiotomy. I crane my head to get a better view. He makes his first cut. Blood comes spurting out.

And I, well, I faint and fall dead away to the floor.

When I come to, I'm on my back on the cold linoleum floor. I'm disoriented, blinking and squinting up at bright lights. A nurse appears, out of the light. At least I think it's a nurse, but she's backlit, like in a movie. She leans over me and waves something under my nose. Smelling salts? I jerk my head from the sharp smell and try to get my bearings. Then the doctor leans into the frame and says, "Schmuck! I have enough problems here. I don't need any more problems with you." And he disappears.

Fainting at the first sight of blood is an indication that perhaps – pardon the pun – I'll never be cut out for a career in medicine. And the reason I'm even in the delivery room is because I'm working at the hospital in the Admissions Department, checking patients in, and I've convinced the doctor to let me see what happens up close. I'm also working at another hospital to support my pre-med studies at UCLA and get more experience.

But on this night, it's not my baby that's going to live or die. It's not my wife that's bringing this baby into the world. I'm trying to give birth to my professional life. The career my parents have chosen for me. A nice, respectable Jewish doctor from Los Angeles. What could be better?

By that point, I had done everything possible to make my parents' dream come true. I'd been an excellent student all through grammar school, middle school and high school. I took Latin. I was class president. I won an American Legion award because of my grades.

Let's Do Launch

When I enrolled at UCLA in January of 1953, I took all the pre-med courses. I wasn't getting all A's like I had in high school, but I was doing okay. Until the second half of my sophomore year, when I received a failing grade on a midterm exam. I'd never had a failing grade in my entire life. The class was Physiology, and it was a red light. A flashing siren. It arrested my attention. Something was wrong.

That failing grade, combined with the fainting episode in the delivery room, told me that maybe I wasn't on the right path after all.

There had to be a better way, and I was determined to find it.

Because I had done all that was prescribed to launch my career as a physician, it was frustrating to feel I was going to have to start all over again.

But I wasn't going to let a little frustration stop me. To my mind, my pre-med "failure" wasn't a failure at all. It revealed a larger obstacle that I, and a lot of people, face when embarking on their career. Namely, what did I want to do with my life?

Figuring this out is not an exact science. There is no GPS that clearly maps out your journey from point A to point B to point C and so on. One person's destination may be the same as someone else, but their paths to get there may substantially differ. To that end, it's reasonable to ask: How do you know what you really want, as opposed to what others want for you – like your parents, your friends or your co-workers? And once you have an idea, where do you start?

These are critical questions to ask. I've seen too many people live, as Thoreau put it, "lives of quiet desperation," trudging along a road that others think is well-suited for them, but they know in their hearts is not. I've seen too many people come to Hollywood thinking they can become overnight successes because they've been told they're attractive and talented and believe it's their destiny – even though they haven't put in the work. And I've seen too many people change jobs or agents or careers because they think they should or because they feel some sort of internal clock "ticking." As a result, they do not get the outcome they want and may cause themselves problems that take them years to unwind.

All too often when people set out upon a journey, be it higher education, a career as an actor or agent, or starting a business, they invest a tremendous amount of resources thinking the sheer size of their investment will guarantee success. For example, a graduating high school senior will go to an expensive university because they and their parents believe the university's name alone will open doors for them. Actors, writers and other talent will switch agents because they think doing so will make them rich and famous. Entrepreneurs will raise money to buy a company because they believe flipping it and becoming a billionaire in five to seven years is a lock.

What this ultimately means is they are at a great risk for spending their time, money and energy like a mouse running on a wheel, endlessly chasing something they'll never catch, and don't want in the first place.

With so much at stake, why do people put themselves in situations that end up costing them so much trouble?

Rags-to-riches, nobody-to-somebody tales of overnight success are the stuff of Hollywood legend. But do tales like this actually happen in the real world?

The answer is yes, but only occasionally.

For every actor, director or writer who gets plucked from obscurity and achieves "instant" fame and fortune, there are millions who make their way to Hollywood only to have their dreams dashed and discarded.

It's not just the artists, either. A generation of ambitious men and women come to Hollywood aspiring to become Ari Gold, the ruthless, egotistical, win-at-any-cost agent played by Jeremy Piven from the hit HBO series, Entourage. The allure of Ari's fast life, and of people like him—access to money, power, fame and everything that goes with them—draws these strivers in, until they discover the reality doesn't always meet the dream.

The myth of overnight success also goes well beyond Hollywood. Bill Gates, Jeff Bezos, Elon Musk and other business luminaries are profiled in glossy magazines because of their entrepreneurial genius and "meteoric" rise to the corner office. However, these examples are few and far between. And for every successful entrepreneur there are a lot more who fail.

It all seems so mysterious and elusive.

But ultimately, by moving away from this notion of overnight success or of the "I'll just shoot from the hip and see what happens" frame of mind, there is a tremendous opportunity to launch yourself and your business in a far more efficient and cost-effective way.

In the next chapter, we'll explore how you discover the sweet spot between what you want, what you're good at, and what people will pay for – whether you're an actor, agent, or entrepreneur.

Chapter 2: What Are You Made Of?

Whether I'm Right Or Whether I'm Wrong
Whether I Find A Place In This World Or Never Belong
I Gotta Be Me, I've Gotta Be Me
What Else Can I Be But What I Am

—Walter Marks
From *Golden Rainbow*

Back at UCLA, after my failing grade in Physiology and my embarrassing fainting episode in the delivery room, I went to the UCLA Counseling Bureau. It was humbling to put myself in the hands of a staff psychologist, but he had been trained to deal with issues like mine — I certainly was not the first student he encountered who did not know what to do — and he put me at ease.

After two or three consultations, he suggested that I take a battery of aptitude and affinity exams to figure out where my interests lay. I was carrying a full course load, and there were about 30 exams, each taking approximately two-hours to complete. Since I could only fit them in when I had some free time, it took me about three or four months to get through them all. After I'd completed everything, the psychologist showed me the results, which were plotted on a graph.

It turned out I had zero interest in any fields of science, and I was quite interested in a completely different area of academics — business, which I had never considered. I immediately switched majors and felt happy with my new direction.

How did this happen? Business wasn't even close to medicine.

As you may recall, it was my parents who wanted me to be a doctor, not me. I was a dutiful son, doing what I was told. And in those days, you didn't resist your parents' wishes.

What's more, as the counselor uncovered in his numerous sessions with me, I felt a lot of pressure. I was the only boy in the family, and I knew that a lot was expected of me. My father's three brothers all had girls, and I was often reminded by my parents and aunts and uncles that I had to perpetuate the name of the Abrams family. I had to become successful in some way, shape or form. Specifically, I had to become a doctor, marry a nice Jewish girl, and have Jewish children.

When the counselor first began probing, I was at first put off by his rather personal line of questioning. But I soon realized he was doing something absolutely critical to help me launch and build a successful life and career. At this critical time of my life, he was taking the time to assess where I was at with my interests and where I wanted to go.

It was a combination of art and science. Subjectivity and objectivity. Dreams and desires coupled with data. The process was thorough and forced me to ask questions of myself that would serve as the foundation for how I'd conduct myself in my life and career. Questions such as: how do you get the right training to prepare yourself? How do you start and structure what you want to do? Do you like working with others or alone? How do you hire people, and let them go? Why is diversity important? Do you want to lead, and if so, what makes a good leader? How do you negotiate? For what do you want to be known? In other words, using today's vernacular, what's your "brand?" How do you take calculated risks, and bounce back from failures? Is there a secret to making it? What does "making it" really mean? Is success all "who you know" rather than what you know? Is success only measured in how much money you make? Do you have to stab people in the back to get ahead? And is "getting ahead" even possible anymore?

The truth is, having a successful career, as well as a fulfilling life, is about a lot more than luck. No matter what field you're in, no matter what circumstances you face, building and sustaining a satisfying life of achievement requires a set of principles, practices, and personal attributes. Chief among them are humility and hunger. The humility to start at the bottom, and the hunger to make it to the top – whatever your "top" is.

I am fortunate to have defied the stereotype of a ruthless egotistical Hollywood mogul and still achieved success in a field everyone can relate to, and everyone has an inherent interest in— entertainment. If I could survive and thrive in that field, surely you can do the same in yours, whatever it may be.

It may seem a bit overwhelming to answer the question of what you'll do with your life. Maybe you're still in high school and you don't know which college is going to be best for you. Perhaps you're about to graduate from a university and can't decide where or with whom to get your first job. Or you could be a few years into your career, and you're thinking about making a change and starting your own company or even switching careers altogether. On top of all that, you may have family and financial considerations to think about that influence the direction your career will take.

Planning your life like this may not be the most enjoyable task you'll ever do, but it is a valuable and necessary step in your journey. To paraphrase Lewis Carroll's *Alice in Wonderland*, if you don't know where you're going, any road will take you there. The good news is there is a way to go about it that can be fascinating, fun, and fruitful.

The first step to understanding where you should go is discovering your strengths. This is what you are *truly* good at, not what you *think* you *might* be good at.

You start with your strengths simply because that's what will produce the best results. And focusing on your weaknesses is a frustrating and demoralizing waste of time.

Thankfully, there are scientifically based methods of going about this. The best I know of is the CliftonStrengths Assessment, a Web-based survey of personality traits from the perspective of positive psychology. As an optimist and positive thinker this appeals to me.

Here's how it works: The CliftonStrengths assessment presents 177 items to you, each consisting of a pair of potential self-descriptors, such as "I read instructions carefully" versus "I like to jump right into things."

The descriptors are placed as if anchoring polar ends of a continuum. You are then asked to choose the descriptor that best describes you, and to identify the extent to which that chosen option is descriptive of you.

You are given 20 seconds to respond to a given pair of descriptors before the assessment automatically presents the next pair. This is so you can't try to outthink the questionnaire and engineer the results you think you should have.

The assessment measures your talents – your natural patterns of thinking, feeling and behaving – and categorizes them into 34 themes within four domains: strategic thinking, executing, influencing, and relationship building.

The themes tell you what kind of strategic thinker, executer, influencer, and relationship builder you are.

For instance, as a strategic thinker, do you like to analyze? Provide context? Seek input? Predict the future? Use your intellect? Generate ideas? Learn?

As a relationship builder, are you adaptable? Do you value harmony? Connectedness? Empathy? Do you like to develop? Include? Relate? Go it alone? Is positivity attractive to you?

What kind of influencer are you? Do you activate? Command? Communicate? Compete? Maximize? Woo? Is self-assurance important to you? How about significance?

How do you execute? Through achievement? By arrangement? Belief? Consistency? Deliberation? Discipline? Focus? Responsibility? Restoration?

Together, the themes explain a simple but profound element of human behavior: what's *right* with people. It's about the strengths you can utilize, not the weaknesses you need to strengthen.

Individually, each theme gives you a way to describe what you naturally do best or what you might need help from others to accomplish.

It's important to understand that finishing the assessment is just the start of finding your role and fulfilling your purpose in life. In order to get the most out of the assessment you need to get Gallup's customized reports and guides to help you interpret the findings and chart your course. Finally, many people also hire a Gallup-Certified Strengths Coach to help them unlock their potential and succeed in every facet of life.

I should say here that I have no connection to the Gallup organization and no financial interest in their company. In fact, they don't even know they're appearing in this book. In all likelihood, there are other outfits that do what they do. But in my experience, they're the best, and I encourage everyone to go through their assessment.

If you think this is too much navel gazing think again. The themes are the culmination of decades of research led by the psychologist and professor Don Clifton to study and categorize the talents of the world's most successful people.

Over the course of his career Clifton published three seminal books on leveraging strengths to set goals and direction: *Soar with Your Strengths*; *Now, Discover Your Strengths*; and *How Full Is Your Bucket?* And in 1999, when he created the CliftonStrengths Assessment and put it online, he made the power of this self-discovery available worldwide.

Imagine if my UCLA counselor had this tool in his arsenal when I went to see him as a student. Or my guidance counselor in high school. I could have saved myself the embarrassment of fainting in the delivery room of the hospital and the frustration of trying to become the doctor I was never meant to be. He did the best he could with what he had, but I know he would have chomped at the bit to use this tool.

Chapter 3: What Have You Done?

Well, that's the first thing you gotta learn,
headlines don't sell papers. Newsies sell papers

—Harvey Fierstein
From *Newsies*

If I'd been more self-aware when I met with the UCLA counselor,
I would have realized life had already given me plenty of clues about
where my strengths and interests lay – and where they didn't.

But that would have required me to look backwards. And as a
young and ambitious guy in a hurry I wasn't much interested in
looking at where I'd been. In fact, before my strengths assessment I
didn't have much use for introspection at all. I did what was in front
of me and figured the future would take care of itself.

There's a lot to be said for living in the moment, and for being
present. I try to live that way myself. But there is a time and a place
for taking stock of where you've been and what you've done. If nothing
else, doing so can boost your self-confidence and remind you of how
capable you are.

A good time to look back is when you're about to embark on your
career journey.

For instance, it would have been useful for me to realize I'd been
working and making money since I was six or seven years old. If I had,
it wouldn't have been such a surprise to be told I should be in business
instead of medicine.

I began by cutting our family's lawn and doing other odd jobs
around the house to make money. I charged a nickel a week in

allowance, and a few weeks later, in the first deal I ever renegotiated – a harbinger of things to come – I got the price up to a quarter.

Then, when I was about eight years old my father said I needed to get a job.

"You mean, besides the stuff I do around here?" I asked.

"Yes," he said. "Money's tight, and anyway, you need to learn the value of a dollar."

"But dad," I said. "I'm eight years old. How am I going to get a job?"

We were sitting at the dinner table. My father at one end, my mother, the other. My sisters and I were on opposite sides, in our customary spots.

Between bites, he said, "Harry, you're going to be in the newspaper business."

My sisters snickered.

My mother admonished them with a sharp "Girls!"

"Newspapers?" I asked. "Like you?"

My father worked in print shops for the local newspapers: *The Los Angeles Times*, the *Herald Express*, the *Los Angeles Daily Mirror*, and the *Los Angeles Examiner* among them. Times were tough, and he bounced between jobs, sometimes going for long stretches of time without any work, other times working two or three jobs at the same time.

"No, my boy," he said. "You're going to be a newspaper man. A real media mogul."

My mother smiled at me sweetly.

"Like Citizen Kane?" I asked. Orson Welles' film, Citizen Kane, in which he played a wealthy media tycoon, had come out a couple of years before that. Although I of course hadn't seen the film, I knew all about it.

"Nope, even better," he said. "Things didn't turn out so well for Charles Foster Kane."

"What am I going to do?"

"You're going to get on your bicycle, deliver newspapers to people's houses, and collect their money."

He made it sound like the most important job in the world, and to me, it was. I delivered two afternoon newspapers and one morning newspaper to families and collected their monthly subscription fees. I kept a logbook of who paid, who didn't pay, and how much people owed. At certain intervals I turned the money into the newspaper offices and got paid. I don't recall how much I earned for delivering each paper, but I remember if I made $25 a month, I considered myself rich.

When I turned nine years old, I got the idea that I could make even more money if I also sold papers on the street corner. So, after my normal paper route I went from my house on Orange Drive, near Venice Boulevard and La Brea Boulevard, picked up more newspapers, went to the intersection of Pico Boulevard and La Brea, and set up shop.

At my street corner – I called it my street corner – when the signal turned red and the traffic stopped, I'd go out into the two traffic lanes and approach the cars. I'd smile, introduce myself, and ask them to buy a paper. I even began to develop a clientele because the same people looked forward to seeing me. I'd cheerfully say, "Nice to see you," and when I got to know their names, I added Mr. Johnson or Mrs. Smith or whatever their names were. Then, before I even got to their window, they'd happily call out, "Harry, where's my newspaper?"

I built up the street corner until I was making good money for an eight-year-old in those years. I couldn't tell you exactly how much, but it seemed like a fortune to me.

So, I expanded.

I had noticed about half a mile down Pico Boulevard, no one was selling newspapers at the intersection of Pico and Redondo Blvds.

I was about 10 years old at that point, and I hired a nine-year-old boy who was a buddy of mine from my neighborhood on Orange Drive. His name was Joel, and he took over my corner at Pico and La Brea, and I went down to the next corner at Pico and Redondo. Now I had two street corners, a paper route, and odd jobs around the house.

I had momentum! I was a going concern! I was going to be rich!

So, I opened a third corner, on Pico and Hauser Blvds., and ran that. I hired another nine-year-old to run the corner I'd just built up. His name was Mel, and he was also from my neighborhood.

Down the street there was a Thrifty Drug Store that was open until midnight. In addition to my three street corners, on Saturday nights from in front of the store, I sold the Sunday issue of the Los Angeles Times that was coming out the next day.

You might think my parents would wonder what they'd unleashed. I mean, here I was this 10-year-old knucklehead selling newspapers all over the place, with actual employees, when I could have been doing anything else. But I loved it, and we really needed the money.

I found out how much we needed it when my father said to me, again at the dinner table, "Harry, you're going to have to start paying rent."

I didn't understand. I was only 10 years old. I was saving my money. I wasn't spending it on candy or comic books or other stupid things.

When I looked to my mother, she wasn't smiling this time, and the girls weren't snickering, either. My father was serious.

As it happened, I was making good money. Plus, from time to time, he was out of a job. I didn't know why that was, especially since there were all kinds of newspapers in those days, and he printed many of them. But I didn't ask questions. I just turned over a portion of my monthly earnings to him.

When I turned 13 years old, I experienced my first business divestiture, so to speak.

Here's how it happened. My family wasn't very religious, but according to Jewish law, when a Jewish boy turns 13, he becomes accountable for his actions and has a bar mitzvah, thus making him a full-fledged adult member of the Jewish community. This was important to my parents, and my buddies were all doing it, so I did it. Afterwards, I couldn't see how a newly minted man who had recently come of age could ride around on a bicycle delivering papers and selling them to people in cars on street corners.

That's when I sold the "rights" to my paper route and my street corners to one of the other kids on the block.

Profit in hand, I ramped up my lawn-cutting business, working after school and on weekends. I also answered phones, filed, and ran errands for different offices. And in one of my more interesting part-time jobs, I worked at North American Aviation.

At the aviation company, from four in the afternoon until midnight, I analyzed employee suggestions and then calculated or computed what savings could conceivably result to the company after their suggestions have been put into effect. And then I had to pitch the idea to management or to the department head. If they implemented the employee's suggestion and it saved the company money, the employee received a cash award. That was one of the best jobs I had.

But when I talked with the counselor at UCLA, none of these jobs inspired me to say, "Business! This is what I should have been doing!" I only looked at those jobs as a way to earn money to help my parents and maybe have a little extra for me.

A career in entertainment hadn't occurred to me, either. I loved going to see plays and musicals with my mother when I was growing up. But making a living in the industry was not even a remote thought when I spoke to the UCLA counselor.

When I opened myself up to inspection, I opened my mind to possibilities.

The more I thought about it, the more I realized I'd started my entertainment career already. When I was about eight or nine years old, I took tap dancing and drama lessons at a local workshop. I played Tom Sawyer in one play, and one of the Peppers – I don't remember which one – in a musical called *The Five Little Peppers* based on the Margaret Sidney book series.

I was even on the radio; *The Great Gildersleve*, live on NBC. My agent – yes, I had an agent; he was from the Meglin Kiddies Agency – got me the part of Leroy, who was a friend of the Gildersleeve Family from the same block. I remember it was a half-hour Christmas show, I had maybe three or four lines, and I blew them. That was the beginning and end of my radio career.

I also worked in a few movies. One was an MGM film called *Big City* with Danny Thomas, Robert Preston, Margaret O'Brien, Butch Jenkins and George Murphy. Danny Thomas played a rabbi, and I sang in his choir.

Another was a United Artists film called *The Diary of a Chambermaid*. I remember it was about a chambermaid who plots to climb the social ladder by marrying a wealthy man. The film starred Paulette Goddard and Burgess Meredith and featured Irene Ryan, who later went on to play "Granny" in the television series *The Beverly Hillbillies*.

The third and final picture I acted in was a United Artists film called *The Strange Woman*. It was set in the 1820s in Maine, in New England. In the film, a beautiful but poor and manipulative woman marries a rich old man, seduces the man's son, then convinces the son to kill his father. It starred Hedy Lamarr, George Sanders and Louis Hayward.

I was only in a few scenes, but that experience convinced me I didn't want to be an actor anymore. Plus, I was about 12 years old at the time, and kids of that age often try things and move on quickly, as I did.

In one scene, Hedy Lamarr's character is a young girl, I'm one of her boyfriends, and we're at a lake in Maine. Actually, it was filmed at Samuel Goldwyn Studios in Hollywood. They built a stage with a lake and a dock that went out into the water. As I'm talking with the young Hedy, she pushes me into the water to drown me. I guess she got started early in the murdering business.

Anyway, I hated it. I had to wear tight wool pants. And if there's anything I hated more than liver and peas, it was wool. I didn't like wool, and worse than wool on your skin was wet wool. I have to wear these tight wool pants, I'm trying to deliver the lines, and I'm twitching. It was itchy. I was scratching. It was terrible. And we had to do it over and over and over.

The worst part were the scenes that took place on the shore of the lake afterwards. Since I'd already been in the water, they needed to make the wool pants look like they were still wet. To do that, they dipped them in oil. With tight, wet, oily and itchy wool pants I'd had enough.

Mercifully, when the film eventually came out, most of my work ended up on the cutting room floor.

During all this time – the radio show, the plays and musicals, the three films – I also kept going to school, of course. Since I was so busy shooting these pictures, and I couldn't go to my regular school, I attended class at the school the production studios ran for child actors. I remember I sat between Elizabeth Taylor and Natalie Wood when I was shooting *Big City* at MGM, and even though I was sandwiched between those two magnificent beauties I still didn't want to be an actor.

But I did develop a deep and abiding love of the theatre — although not as an actor — in the Los Angeles of my youth. I saw a lot of plays and musicals at community theaters, high schools, and colleges. Most of all, I went downtown to the Biltmore Theater, which for 40 years was the premier venue for touring Broadway shows playing Los Angeles. The theatre was connected by walkways on the east and south sides to the Biltmore Hotel.

To me, the Biltmore Theater was another wonder of the world, equal to the Roman Colosseum, the Great Wall of China, and the Great Pyramid of Giza. As a boy, when I walked into the lobby I was overwhelmed by the polish and beauty, both in the building itself and of the theater attendees who were dressed in their finest. It was hard not to trip and fall as I made my way to my seat, my mouth hanging open as I gazed at the setting. The Biltmore had 1,652 seats, three balconies, and a huge proscenium stage. And in that space — that hallowed ground — when the huge curtains opened and the lights went down, magic took place.

The Biltmore opened in 1924 — 11 years before I was born — with a production of Jerome Kern's *Sally*, starring Leon Errol, Walter Catlett, and Shirley Vernon. None other than Will Rogers conducted the opening night ceremonies. Over the next four decades Biltmore audiences, including me, saw such stars as Katherine Cornell, Alfred Lunt and Lynne Fontanne, Helen Hayes, Tallulah Bankhead, Gertrude Lawrence, Judith Anderson, Al Jolson, and the Marx Brothers.

On April 25, 1964, due to unsustainable expenses and taxes, the Biltmore Theater closed its spectacular curtains for the last time as Joseph Stein's *Enter Laughing* with Yvonne DeCarlo, Alan Mowbray, and Alan Arkin finished a 23-week run.

In the May 3, 1964 edition of the Los Angeles Times, the very paper I'd delivered 20 years earlier, James Dolittle, general director of the Biltmore Association, said with the completion of the Huntington Hartford Theater and the Los Angeles Music Center, the Biltmore Theater would no longer be needed.

I was heartbroken, and I didn't see how anything could take its place.

Nothing did for more than 20 years because the Biltmore was demolished in 1964, and a parking lot went up in its place.

When Joni Mitchell wrote "they paved paradise to put up a parking lot" in her song *Big Yellow Taxi* a few years later, she was referring to a massive parking lot she saw from her hotel window in Honolulu. Surrounded by beauty, she called the parking lot a "blight on paradise," and sat down to write the song.

She might as well have written it about the space where the Biltmore Theater had been.

However, all was not lost as Joseph Stein followed *Enter Laughing* with a little show called *Fiddler on the Roof* that same year, and I would one day serve on the board of directors for the Los Angeles Fraternity of Friends, a fundraising organization attached to the very same Music Center of Los Angeles that influenced the demise of the Biltmore Theatre.

Life comes full circle.

And the answer to where had I been was just what the UCLA counselor had revealed: I'd been working all my life, I'd already been an entrepreneur at an early age, and I loved the entertainment industry.

Chapter 4: Where Do You Want To Go??

Every man has his daydreams
Every man has his goal
People like the way dreams have
Of sticking to the soul

—Stephen Schwartz
From *Pippin*

At this point you've taken the CliftonStrengths assessment or worked with your school counselor or if you're already in your career you've gotten insight from some trusted associates.

You've taken a look back at the work you've done and the life experiences you've had so far.

You now better understand what you like and don't like.

So what do you do? How do you plot a course for your future?

My advice is to begin with your destination in mind, and then work backwards, to where you currently are. Make a list of the steps you need to take to reach your destination. Which will probably start with getting a good college education. If you want to be an actor, do you go to a drama school like Yale or the Royal Academy of Dramatic Art (RADA)? If you want to be a director or producer or screenwriter, do you go to NYU or USC? What if you want to become a talent agent? Do you go to Harvard or UCLA to get an MBA or law degree first? Aside from school, what other training do you need?

Like points on a map, write these stops down. Then, systematically take them, making sure to adjust your course as needed.

In my case, it was my UCLA counselor who initiated my change in direction from medical school to business when he said, "You know, you could go on and continue in pre-med and maybe be lucky enough to get into medical school. But even if you graduate from medical school at some point, you're not going to be a doctor. From a career standpoint, you'd probably go into some other form of work such as advising physicians what to do with their money or becoming a hospital administrator."

When I asked him what I should do he said, "Well, your test results show you're interested in all forms of business – accounting, finance, sales, marketing, public relations, advertising, manufacturing, business law, management, entrepreneurship. You also have a tremendous amount of interest in, and knowledge of, the entertainment industry. If what you study has anything to do with business and entertainment, I think you'll thrive. You should change your major to business administration right away."

Business and entertainment. Hmm. Since I had no artistic abilities, I wasn't a writer, I wasn't a director, and I wasn't an actor – the incident with the tight, wet, oily and itchy wool pants proved that – I decided I'd have to be behind the scenes.

I did a lot of research. I spoke to a lot of people. And I came to the conclusion that, although I didn't know in what capacity I'd work, it would indeed be in entertainment.

With that in mind, I had my destination.

For my first step in this new journey, I had to fulfill a military obligation. In addition to working odd jobs to pay for UCLA, I was in the Reserve Officers' Training Corps (ROTC) which gave me a scholarship for committing to serve in the United States Army for six months once I graduated. I would enter the army as a commissioned officer, a second lieutenant.

I was going to be farther away from Los Angeles than I'd ever been, and a world away from the entertainment industry. But it's what I had signed up for, and I was determined I'd make the most of the experience.

Off I went to six weeks of basic training as a medical service corps officer (MSC) at Fort Sam Houston in San Antonio, Texas. Perhaps the medical service corps designation was a holdover from my pre-med studies. I don't know. In any case, at basic training, I learned some great skills, did what I was told, and got in the best shape of my life. As an ancillary benefit, I got a great tan working in the sun. As anyone who knows me is aware, I love the sun and I like having a healthy glow.

After basic training I became a public information officer at the Brooke Army Medical Center (BAMC) which was also at Fort Sam Houston. The BAMC is the Department of Defense's largest in-patient hospital, its only Level 1 trauma center, and home to the Center for the Intrepid, an outpatient rehabilitation facility. More than 8,000 soldiers, airmen, sailors, civilians and contractors work there providing care to wounded service members and the San Antonio community at large.

I lived in the bachelor officer quarters and loved it as much as any 22-year-old single male can. Besides going out at night, I thoroughly enjoyed my job. As the Post spokesperson and liaison with magazines, newspapers, radio, and television, I wrote press releases, ran press conferences, and went to lunches and dinners on behalf of the military. The experience taught me skills I use to this day. How to speak in public. How to get along with members of the press and the entertainment community who came to the Post. How to work with colleagues as a peer, as a leader, and as someone who reported to leaders. When to take initiative and balance risks with rewards. How to manage a budget. How to act for the greater good instead of for myself. How to be on time, and accountable. How to keep my word, and act ethically. How to negotiate so not only you win, but everyone wins.

Everything in my experience at Fort Sam Houston has been critical to my career as a talent agent and business owner. I'd even say it was all important in my development as a person.

I say this because I believe there are no ordinary moments in life. All of our experiences provide us with opportunities to learn valuable lessons. We have to be open enough to learning, however, and treat education as a life-long pursuit. We have to be willing to make mistakes and learn from them. Because life will keep giving us the lesson until we get it right.

Having fulfilled my obligation to the military, armed with a vague notion that I wanted to be on the business side of entertainment, I set off to conquer the world.

But first, I had to get a job. However, like millions of college graduates who have come before and after me, finding a job would prove to be a lot harder than I thought it would be.

Chapter 5: Stay Humble and Hungry

You learn to speak so calmly when
Your heart would like to scream and shout.
You learn to stop and breathe and smile
You learn to live without.

—Brian Yorkey and Thomas Robert Kitt
From *If/Then*

For a long time after I'd gone into entertainment, my parents thought I'd made the wrong decision. Until 10 or 15 years later, when I was at Abrams-Rubaloff & Associates, when I brought my mother and my father into my office and let them spend a good eight-hour day with me. Each one separately. One the first day, the other the next day. I wanted to show them how happy I was, and how what I had decided on had become such a success.

I showed them that despite my change in direction, I was still practicing medicine. They saw how I dealt with egotistic executives from advertising agencies. How I worked with complicated actors and performers. How I helped performers guide their careers and make choices and decisions, and how, as artists they could be challenging to deal with.

Upon witnessing me at work, my father said, "Harry, from what I see, you can hang a shingle outside your office right now that says 'Harry Abrams, M.D.' because these people are nuts and you're their psychiatrist."

But the distance between Fort Sam Houston and Abrams-Rubaloff & Associates was still light years away.

Before going into the military, when I was still at UCLA, one of my best friends at the fraternity I was in, ZBT, was Bill Ziv. Like a few of the guys in the fraternity, Bill's father was in entertainment. His name was Fred Ziv, and he owned Ziv Television Productions. I went with Bill to visit his dad at the studio periodically.

As time went on, Bill's dad took a liking to me. He told me after I got out of the military, he'd find a job for me somewhere within his company. Not quite the "overnight success" of Hollywood dreams, but pretty close.

However, when I arrived back in Los Angeles, ready to start my entertainment career, I discovered there wasn't going to be a job for me after all. The country had fallen on hard times, and as a result, there simply weren't any jobs to be had, much less in the entertainment industry.

With the rent due on the apartment I had rented, and no job to support myself because the one I'd been promised failed to materialize, I got a job as a part-time delivery boy with Thrifty Drug Store in Beverly Hills.

I hustled making deliveries all over Los Angeles in my beat-up old car and got to know the back streets and alleys. I still know those streets. To this day, many of my friends tell stories about riding in my car as I carry on a conversation and drive them to the Staples Center for Laker games. I have season's tickets in the fourth row because Chick Hearn, the voice of the Lakers, was my client for many years. But when I was a delivery boy from Thrifty, well, those were lean times.

To save money, I used to get free haircuts from my grandfather, who was one of the three barbers at 20th Century Fox studios. It was nothing for me to sit patiently while my grandfather cut the hair of Tyrone Power or Gregory Peck or some other big star. When he had time, I'd jump in the chair.

My grandfather knew I wanted to get into the entertainment business. But one day, he shocked me when he called me at home.

"Harry," he said. "You know who Spyros Skouras is?"

"Yes," I replied. "He's the chairman and CEO of 20th Century Fox. Why?"

"Well, Mr. Skouras is flying in from New York that morning, and I'm going to give him a haircut here in the barbershop."

"That's neat," I said.

"Why don't you come over here and meet Mr. Skouras?" he said. "I'll be cutting his hair, and perhaps afterward, if we do this right before lunch, he'll invite us to eat with him in the executive dining room, and maybe there might be a job that could ensue."

Before I could consider the utter audacity of the idea, I got myself together and hurried to the barbershop. By the time I arrived, my grandfather had already spoken to Mr. Skouras, who had offered to take us to lunch in the executive dining room at 20th Century Fox.

Here's my poor immigrant grandfather, who came to the United States from Russia, imposing himself upon this. . .this Greek god. He was the head of 20th Century Fox – all of it – and to me, that made him bigger than the president of the United States. If I'd had time to think about the chutzpah it took for my grandfather to ask for this meeting, let alone get it, I would have been scared out of my mind.

What I didn't know, was that my grandfather had been talking about me to Mr. Skouras for quite some time. He was a lot smarter than I gave him credit for.

Before I can blink, my grandfather and I are in the executive dining room with Mr. Skouras. We have a terrific lunch, and Mr. Skouras talks with me at length about the company, and about the entertainment industry. It's like a master class, except over lunch. As we finish, he stuns me with what he says next.

"Harry, I have a secretary who is permanently here in Los Angeles at 20th Century Fox," he says. "His name is John Healy. He takes care of me beautifully. But at the moment I don't have a traveling secretary. You know, someone who flies around the world with me and keeps things running smoothly, just like Mr. Healy does here. Would you be interested in filling that role with me, and being my traveling secretary?"

I'm flabbergasted. Inside, I'm screaming, "Are you kidding!? I'm a part-time delivery boy at a Thrifty Drug Store, I want to get into entertainment, and you're offering me a position flying around the world with the chairman and CEO of 20th Century Fox!?"

But I keep my composure and say, "Yes. I would love to do that, Mr. Skouras."

"That's terrific," he says. "Just one thing, do you know Gregg shorthand? I dictate a lot."

"No, I do not," I say. "However, I can go to school and learn it very quickly."

"Well, why don't you investigate that?" he says.

Then, all of a sudden, his secretary, John Healy, enters the dining and comes straight over to Mr. Skouras, who introduces us. I don't know how Mr. Healy knows to appear at this precise moment. Maybe Mr. Skouras has somehow signaled him? Is he that powerful?

"You stay in touch with Mr. Healy, and let him know what your progress is," he says. "As soon as you finish your course in shorthand, we'll make arrangements for you to join the company."

I walked out on a cloud, virtually flew home, and found a course in the yellow pages – the same kind of yellow pages I'd printed with my father in one of my part-time jobs a few years earlier. I called the company who offered the course, told them my situation, and convinced them to squeeze their three-month curriculum into six weeks.

Once a week for the next month I called Mr. Healy to let him know how I was doing. Things were moving along quite expeditiously when I got a call one day about four weeks into the process. It was Mr. Healy telling me that Mr. Skouras had decided he couldn't wait any longer and had already hired someone.

I was devastated. If he could have waited two more weeks, I'd have finished the course and been able to join him. I never found out why he couldn't wait or why I didn't get something else with 20th Century Fox, especially since I'd worked so hard to get in there. Maybe some guy with an Ivy league education got the job. Could have been a pretty girl. Or perhaps it was a relative, one of his children or nieces or nephews or something. Any of those scenarios is a common occurrence in Hollywood.

I know my grandfather was disappointed, and he said he understood. But it would have made him so happy and proud to think that through his efforts – talking to Mr. Skouras, introducing me – he could help me get a job doing what I wanted to do.

Bottom line: it wasn't going to happen.

This meant that in rapid succession, I'd experienced my first two entertainment industry heartbreaks. The first was not getting a job with Ziv Television Productions after I'd been promised it upon my return from military service. The second was not getting this job with 20th Century Fox after I'd been promised it upon my learning Gregg shorthand.

To say I was humbled is a vast understatement. But I was also something else: hungry. Not physically hungry. Professionally hungry. And I was being given a test millions of people fail at every day. Would I give up and settle for less or would I keep pushing?

I dug in, and I pushed.

With my eyes on my goal of getting into entertainment, I began to apply for a position in the talent agency business. I thought it would be a good experience to learn all about the entertainment industry and to be behind the scenes as a talent agent. I'd read a lot about it. I'd talked to enough people about it. So I did it.

I applied for jobs in the mailrooms of two agencies, Music Corporation of America, also known as MCA, and the William Morris Agency. They both had agent training programs that would require me to start in the mailroom. The pay was $40 a week, and I wanted that job.

Again, I had no entry into the business. Again, I had no contacts. And again, I forged ahead. I researched who the personnel directors were at those agencies, wrote two good letters of inquiry, and sent them off. In addition, I enclosed photocopies of all the letters I'd collected from the previous jobs I'd had. Thinking ahead, every time I'd left a job I asked for a letter of recommendation. I put those letters to use hoping they might help me get noticed by those personnel directors. I looked for any edge I could get.

A few weeks later I got calls from both MCA and the William Morris Agency. They wanted me to come in for interviews. I was elated. But I tempered my enthusiasm somewhat because of my previous disappointments.

The first person I met with was Earl Zook at MCA. Earl had been an accountant for Pan American Petroleum, and again for Warner Brothers, before he became Jules Stein and Lew Wasserman's personnel director at MCA.

At William Morris I initially met with a friend from high school and college, Joe Wizan. Joe had started in the mailroom at William

Morris a few years earlier. Like me, he had also graduated from UCLA and served in the military before entering the entertainment industry.

The process at both agencies were similar. After you met with the personnel directors, if they felt you were of sufficient caliber and perhaps someone who might appeal to them for their agent training program, you'd move along to the next step, which was being interviewed by different department heads at the respective agencies. This meant you did separate interviews with the heads of the motion picture, television, personal appearance, literary and commercial departments. These were people in senior management who had a lot of influence over who might be extended an opportunity to come into the training program.

Another part of the process was that at any point along the way, you could be rejected and turned away if just one of the interviewers, for whatever reason, felt you shouldn't be in the program. It was kind of like entering a fraternity at a university. A hazing, if you will. Another way to look at it; it was like an actor auditioning for a part in a play or film or television show. Everyone is as smart and talented and attractive and ambitious and charming as you are – and you can be rejected for anything.

It was stressful to have to run the gauntlet of people who had what you wanted, had professional power over you, and could impact your career, positively and negatively, with a nod of their head or a dismissive note scrawled in a margin. They were people in their 40s, 50s or 60s who had grown up within the agency and were at the peak of their career. Powerful and influential talent agents like Arthur Park, Herman Citron, George Chasin, Berle Adams, Mickey Rockford, Michael Levee, Eddie Green, Don Fishel, Monique James and Ina Bernstein. When you're 22 or 23 years of age, and you're going up against this lineup, it's as if you're facing Babe Ruth, Lou Gehrig, and the rest of the 1927 New York Yankees.

Still, I always wanted to speed up the process. But of course, I knew I had to move at their speed, and patiently wait for the telephone to ring before I could proceed.

The interview period lasted about three months between the two agencies. Finally, after meeting with more than 25 people, I received calls from the personnel directors at MCA and William Morris. They told me I had finished the interviews.

I said, "Terrific! Do I have a job?"

And they both replied in the same way. "Well, your name will be placed on a list of approved applicants. We have several applicants who have been through the same process and whose names are on the list ahead of you. When your name rises to the top of the list, we'll call you. We'll let you know."

"Should I check in from time to time?"

"No. Do not call. We'll call you."

"Okay," I said. "Do you have any idea when this will occur?"

"No, we couldn't tell you."

"Is it weeks?" I asked. "Months? Years?"

The answer was curt this time. "Young man, we don't know. It depends on if or when we'll have the need if we expand or add people to the company. We will have to see if or when an opportunity presents itself."

I knew I was pressing my luck. "That sounds good to me," I chirped. "Whenever you do call, I'll be ready. Thank you for the opportunity."

And that was it. In addition to the uncertainty in my situation, and the pressure from my parents to get a "real job," the country was in the midst of a recession. The economy was so bad the trade papers reported that 200,000 people in the entertainment industry were out of work.

Besides waiting by the phone – patience was not exactly one of my virtues – what was I supposed to do? Better yet, to paraphrase Sean Connery in *The Untouchables*, "What was I prepared to do?"

Chapter 6: Defer the Dream

There's a million things I haven't done
well, just you wait, just you wait.

—Lin-Manuel Miranda
From *Hamilton*

It's 1958, I've twice tried and failed to get a job in the entertainment industry – with the third try hanging by a thread – and I'm still a 23-year-old part-time delivery boy at a local drug store. To top it off, the Thrifty Drug Store at which I'm working is in Beverly Hills, so I am surrounded by wealthy people. Which I most certainly am not.

After graduating from a premier university like UCLA and serving as the spokesperson for one of the country's largest Army bases, that was not how I wanted to start my career.

A lot of people would get down in the dumps and wait for the phone to ring. And really, who could blame them?

I decided to take a different approach. While keeping my eyes on the prize, i.e., the mailroom at MCA or William Morris, I was going to look for a position outside of entertainment. I came to the realization that sometimes you have to look beyond instant gratification and play the long game. You have to temporarily defer your dream. That didn't mean I was giving up or hedging my bet. It meant I was widening my field of opportunity.

I turned to my uncle, Henry Harvey. Married to my mother's sister, my Aunt Fran, Uncle Henry was a housewares buyer for the Thrifty Drug Store chain. He helped me get the delivery boy job, and I looked up to him for his business acumen.

Among the items Uncle Henry bought for Thrifty were power lawn mowers, from the G. W. Davis Power Lawn Mower Manufacturing Company. He knew the owner, Maury Lober, very well since he came to Los Angeles often. They had about 150 workers at their factory in Indiana, where they manufactured lawn mowers in two eight-hour shifts.

The next time Mr. Lober was in town my uncle took me to lunch to meet him. By the end of the lunch Mr. Lober said if I would be willing to leave Los Angeles and move to Richmond, Indiana, where his company was based, I could work for him as his assistant.

"Would you do that?" he asked. "Would you leave the glamour of Hollywood for the corn fields of Indiana?"

This was a long way from traveling around the world with Spyros Skouras, working in television production for Fred Ziv, or representing movie stars. Then again, none of those things had happened. Although I wanted to work in Hollywood as much as ever, this was a job, a real job, and it was right in front of me. And of course, I had studied manufacturing and business at UCLA's School of Business Administration, so I figured I knew a thing or two.

I sat up straight, looked him in the eye, and said, "Mr. Lober, that would be terrific." Then we shook hands to seal the deal.

With the exception of going to San Antonio, where I was in the Army, and to Las Vegas once in a while when I was at UCLA, I had really never been outside of Los Angeles. This was going to be an exciting adventure for me to go to Richmond, Indiana.

I packed a few things, flew from Los Angeles to Indianapolis, and drove to Richmond in a rented car. Richmond, Indiana was a small town off route 70 – which runs from Maryland to Utah – and it was right on the Ohio and Indiana border. Indianapolis was 73 miles to the west, Cincinnati was 73 miles to the south, and Dayton, Ohio was 53 miles west to the east. I was going from Los Angeles, with a population of around six million people, to Richmond, which had about 40,000 people. Quite a change for a city kid.

On the same day I arrived I rented a tiny one-bedroom house close to the factory. The next morning, I went to work. Technically, I reported to the president of the company, Harold Lowenstein. But since

Mr. Lowenstein lived in Cincinnati and only came up to the factory three days a week, I mostly answered to the factory superintendent.

As the only college graduate among 150 rough and tough factory workers, from liberal Los Angeles, of all places, I had to figure out how to fit in. This meant listening to a lot of country music, and hearing people talk about hunting and fishing and bowling and drinking beer. It meant putting aside any preconceived notions I might have about who these guys were and what they thought about life. It also meant being myself, because no one likes a phony. Learning how to fit in, and yet still be myself, is a skill that has helped me for my entire career. It has helped me understand people, have empathy, and develop a rapport where I might otherwise have not thought possible.

I had a myriad of responsibilities, and it seemed like it was non-stop. In a nutshell, my job involved everything and anything that involved the assembling and manufacturing of power lawn mowers — the kind that you push, not the kind that you ride.

For instance, as the person in charge of purchasing I bought all the items that went into the assembling of the lawn mower. Steel housing. Blades. Rubber tires. Aluminum tubing that went from the housing to the handles. The engines; three-quarter horsepower, one horsepower, and four horsepower. Nuts. Screws. Bolts. Paint. Everything.

It was as far from entertainment as I could have gotten, and I loved it.

Plus, I was making about $125 a week, which was a fortune to me in those days. Especially since the jobs I applied for at MCA and William Morris only paid $40 a week. I'd never seen that kind of money before. I thought I was rich.

I was also in charge of warehousing and inventory control. This meant I had to deal with railroads and freight companies, and not only keep track of everything I purchased, but know what was on hand and where at any given time. The company had salesman all over the country selling these power mowers. I took a steady stream of orders over the Telex machine, and if I didn't have the purchasing and inventory down pat the entire operation would grind to a halt. It was fascinating and exciting to have that much responsibility.

One day, after I'd spent almost a year in Indiana, my parents called to tell me I received a letter from the William Morris Agency. I asked them to open the letter and read it to me. They said the William Morris Agency had a position open for $40 a week, and it was mine if I wanted it. The personnel director, with whom I'd check in every couple of months, gave me 72 hours to accept the position or not. If I didn't take the job, he said he'd move on to the next person on the list, and I'd be removed from contention.

I thought back to the months I'd spent interviewing at MCA and William Morris, and how I had come to know the department heads. After observing them closely, I'd come to the conclusion that the people at MCA were significantly more well-informed and savvier than the people at The William Morris Agency. Whether it was true or not, that was my perception.

I called the personnel director at MCA and asked if my name was still on the list. He said it was, but he couldn't tell me when the position would open up. So, I took a calculated risk and turned down the opportunity at The William Morris Agency. Which was something that you just didn't do, and it was very upsetting to my parents. They thought this was my brass ring, and they didn't understand how I could make such a decision.

But I told them that I was doing just fine there. I was earning good money. I was having a terrific time. And I was a single guy living in rural Richmond, Indiana surrounded by pretty farm girls.

After another six months MCA called and said my name had risen to the top of the list. They had a job for me in MCA's mailroom if I wanted it. Like William Morris, it would pay $40 a week. However, unlike William Morris, I only had 24 hours to decide whether I was going to take the job or not. I took the job in a heartbeat.

I'd been waiting anxiously for that position. I'd planned for it. I turned down William Morris for it, and I wasn't going to let it slip away. Plus, aside from the pretty farm girls, I'd had my fill of the Midwest and Richmond, Indiana. I was ready to go home.

When I called Mr. Lober to tell him I was leaving the company he said, "Well, before you leave, let me take you to dinner. Let's talk about this." Mr. Lober, who divided his time between Cincinnati and his apartment on Central Park West in New York City, flew in the next day.

Over dinner, he said he didn't have any children, and I'd become like a son to him. What's more, he said he liked what I was doing and didn't have anyone else who could take my place. Although my salary had increased to about $125 a week at that point he said, "I will double that and pay you $250 a week to stay with the company and take on more responsibility." I said, "Thank you very much, Mr. Lober, but my heart is set on the entertainment industry, and I have an opportunity to get into it, so I have to leave." He was disappointed, and he must have thought twice about my intelligence, but he said he understood.

I made my way back to Los Angeles, to start working at MCA in the mailroom for $40 a week. I was going to be working twice as many hours for about a sixth of the pay. But I was on my way.

Part Two: The Launch

Chapter 7: The Other White House

I know what my people are thinking tonight
As home through the shadows they wander.
Everyone smiling in secret delight
They stare at the castle and ponder.
Whenever the wind blows this way
You can almost hear everyone say
I wonder what the king is doing tonight?

—Alan Jay Lerner and Frederick Loewe
From *Camelot*

Imagine going to the White House and working for the president of the United States. Think what that must have been like for George Stephanopoulos, Jon Favreau or Jen Psaki when they first walked into the White House, found their offices, and went to work for presidents Bill Clinton, Barack Obama and Joe Biden. Each of those young people were already accomplished professionals. But it had to be at least a little intimidating knowing the place where you worked was an international symbol of democracy, and the person for whom you worked was the leader of the free world.

Although at 23 years old – the age at which I joined MCA, in 1958 – I lacked the pedigree and accomplishments of Stephanopoulos, Favreau or Psaki, for me, going to work for Jules Stein and Lew Wasserman in MCA's big white complex at 360 North Crescent Drive in Beverly Hills was like working for President Kennedy and Vice President Johnson in the big white complex at 1600 Pennsylvania Ave in Washington, D.C.

Suffice it to say that the world I was entering was unlike anything I'd ever known.

The name of MCA's co-founder and CEO – Dr. Julian **Caesar** Stein (whom I and everyone else knew simply as Jules Stein) – is emblematic of how people thought of him and how he ran his entertainment empire. Since practicing as an ophthalmologist in 1920s Chicago apparently wasn't enough for his grand ambitions, Stein, with William Goodheart, Jr., in 1924, started a side hustle called Music Corporation of America (MCA). They found and booked musicians for one-night stands and longer engagements for legitimate clubs and illegal speakeasies run by an empire builder of a different sort, the infamous mafia boss, Al Capone. MCA, which began with legendary musicians such as Jelly Roll Morton, King Oliver, Louis Armstrong, Count Basie, Fats Waller and more, grew rapidly and included tours to New York, Dallas, Cleveland, and Los Angeles. Before long the side hustle was front and center.

Meanwhile, between 1926 and 1930, "talkies" began to gradually overtake silent films in Hollywood. Audiences were enamored with musical pictures, where they could hear orchestras play beautiful scores and see stars on the big screen whom they had previously only been able to see on stage. Gangster movies were also popular as audiences enjoyed hearing sound effects such as the rat-a-tat-tat of machine guns, squealing tires, and police car sirens. And of course, music was, pardon the pun, instrumental in heightening the tension.

With MCA already in the music business, and music and talking actors playing such an important role in Hollywood, Stein decided there was money to be made – a lot of money – representing the movie stars who were doing the talking. But he knew he couldn't do it from Chicago. He needed to go to Hollywood. He needed to *move* to Hollywood. And he couldn't do it half-assed. He needed to go *big*, and he needed to have a building that reflected his scheme of conquest. Moreover, Stein wanted to convey an image of old-school sophistication to offset the firm's speakeasy origins.

To design the company's Hollywood home, Stein commissioned master architect Paul Revere Williams, the first African American Fellow of the American Institute of Architects. For his part, Williams wanted to create a statement. He wanted to build something that rivaled the studios in Culver City. He thought, if you want to work with a star you need to *look like* a star. To achieve that, Williams wanted to design a building that was a perfect representation of Hollywood in the '30s. And boy, did he ever.

Located on the southeast corner of North Crescent Drive and "Little" Santa Monica Boulevard, the MCA complex was 124,000 sq.ft. and sat on a 2 1/2-acre complex. It looked like an elaborate film set from one of Hollywood's big movie musicals. Visitors entered through vintage iron gates, and were met with porches, gabled roofs, columns, gardens, statues, a fountain and reflecting pool, and a parking garage. Inside, there were more than 30 offices, a radio station, a projection room, and a hidden bar. Williams chose an English Georgian Revival style because he wanted to create a welcoming atmosphere that conveyed a combination of work and home and status. It was essentially an exclusive club for MCA's clients, and it effectively delivered the message, "This is the establishment. If you're here, you've made it."

This is the new world I was entering. Not an Army base. Not a Thrifty drug store. And certainly not a lawn mower company in the middle of cornfields.

MCA's professional philosophy was equally as important as its physical setting.

When Lew Wasserman joined MCA in 1936 at the age of 23, he and everyone else who ever worked for Jules Stein learned the company's "Rules of the Road." The rules were a codification of how an agent was to conduct their business. While the rules were spiritually carved onto figurative stone tablets, they were augmented over the years to reflect new learnings and practices from successive MCA leaders. Although the rules could apply to just about any business, they amounted to MCA's "secret sauce" and were closely guarded. That is, until 1999, when a version of the rules was revealed by a former MCA agent, Jerry Perenchio, and published in the *Wall Street Journal*. Like me, Jerry was a UCLA graduate, former ROTC member and military officer, albeit for the Air Force. He was five years older than me, but we both joined MCA at around the same time.

These are the "Rules of the Road" upon which Lew Wasserman, Jerry Perenchio, and I, along with generations of other agents have built our careers:

- Stay clear of the press. No interviews, no panels, no speeches, no comments. Stay out of the spotlight — it fades your suit.
- No nepotism, no hiring of friends.
- Never rehire anyone.
- Hire people smarter and better than you. Delegate responsibilities to them. Doing so will make your job easier.
- You've got to know your territory. Cold!
- Do your homework. Be prepared.
- Teamwork.
- Take options, never give them.
- Always ask questions. Don't give answers.
- Rely on your instincts and common sense. If you go against them, you generally regret it.
- No surprises. We don't give them. We don't want to get them.
- Never lose sight of what business you're in. Stick to your "last."
- When you suit up each day it's to play in Yankee Stadium or Dodger stadium. Think big.
- If you have a problem, don't delay. Face up to it immediately and solve it.
- Loose lips sink ships!
- Supreme self-confidence, never arrogance.
- A true leader is accessible — no job too big, no job too small.
- Communication is our business. You can reach any of your associates anytime, anywhere, anyplace.
- If you make a mistake, admit it. Just don't make too many.
- Don't be a "customer's person" (man or woman). You represent your client.
- Always, always take the high road. Be tough but fair and never lose your sense of humor.

Over my six decades in entertainment, I've encountered plenty of eye rolls, grimaces, and muttered sighs of "there goes the old guy sticking to his outdated ways" when I've cited some version of those rules to younger people. But let's look at the success these rules have bred.

Take Jerry Perenchio. The grandson of Italian immigrants, and raised on a farm in Fresno, Jerry worked his way through college doing odd jobs and running his own business – Party Management – that booked bands and catered parties. Although his background gave no hint of his future success, Jerry became the youngest vice president in MCA's history, started his own agency after MCA was forced to break up in 1962, and grew it to become the fifth-largest agency in the world before he sold it to International Creative Management (ICM) in 1972. During the transition of his agency to ICM, Jerry promoted the "Fight of the Century" between Muhammad Ali and Joe Frazier at Madison Square Garden, and with another ICM agent at the time, Alan Morell, who is now chairman and CEO of Creative Management Partners, promoted the "Battle of the Sexes" tennis match between Bobby Riggs and Billie Jean King at the Houston Astrodome.

If that's not enough evidence MCA's credo was critical to his success, consider Jerry's career *after* he left the agency business. He was president and CEO of Tandem Pictures until 1983, when the company was sold to Columbia Pictures. He then founded Castle Rock Entertainment, became president of Warner Brothers, and was chairman of Walt Disney Studios. Finally, in 1992, he bought the Univision network for $550 million and built it into a Fortune 500 company before selling it, in 2007, for $13.5 billion.

Then there's Lew Wasserman himself. Born to Russian immigrants in Cleveland, Ohio, Lew rose from high-school dropout to chairman and CEO of MCA, engineered the takeover of Universal Studios, and probably changed Hollywood more than anyone who has ever lived. By the time his career, which spanned nine decades, was through, two biographies were written about him. *The Last Mogul: The Life and Times of Lew Wasserman*, by Dennis McDougal, and *When Hollywood Had a King: The Reign of Lew Wasserman, Who Leveraged Talent into Power and Influence*, by Connie Bruck.

Speaking to *The Washington Post*, Jack Valenti, former special assistant to President Lyndon Johnson, and the man whom Lew Wasserman installed as President of the Motion Picture Association of America, described him like this: "What you have to understand is if Hollywood is Mount Olympus, Lew Wasserman is Zeus."

I can't say I agree with all of the ways Lew conducted business, and I did not condone how he sometimes treated people. Not just employees, but clients. At 6 feet 3 inches tall and weighing about 160 pounds, with white hair, enormous black glasses, and a conservative dark suit, Lew was an imposing figure. Like Zeus did with lesser gods, Lew could explode into rage-filled tirades that made seasoned and successful executives faint and vomit. He was by turns hated, loved, feared and respected. Although he changed the image of Hollywood agents from cigar-chewing windbags to polished professionals he was truly loathed by some in Hollywood, including Shirley Temple, whom he fired as a client by telling her she was "washed up," and "too old" to play the children's roles that made her famous — and that helped to fill MCA's considerable coffers. Imagine making one of America's most beloved child actors cry, then callously giving her a single tissue as you pushed her out of your office. That's not for me.

While I no doubt had moments as a CEO that were less than inspiring, I never wanted to intentionally emulate the negative aspects of Lew Wasserman's character. Instead, I wanted to produce the kind of results he did, but do it with integrity, optimism, preparation, diversity and inclusion, and a host of other positive attributes. In short, I wanted to improve upon the "Rules of the Road," and make them mine.

Chapter 8: Be Willing to Start at the Bottom

My first month in the mailroom was nothing to write home about.

A main part of the job was picking up and delivering scripts, photographs, films, gifts, invitations and other correspondence. We often used the cars the agency kept outside the mailroom, all of which were gray or charcoal gray, much like the color of the suits everyone wore. It was all conservative and traditional. Even though I was the most recent hire, which meant I was number six out of the six people working in the mailroom, I was excited about being there.

One day, after only two weeks on the job, while the other five guys in the mailroom were out on deliveries or pickups, the phone rang. I'd only encountered Jules Stein a couple of times, but I recognized his gruff voice right away.

He growled, "Who is this?"

"It's Harry Abrams, sir."

He said, "Abrams, you've seen my Mercedes 300SL? Metallic blue?"

"Yes, sir."

"It's sitting outside in the executive parking lot."

"Yes, sir."

He said, "Get it to my house right away. I'm up here on Angelo Drive in Beverly Hills off of Benedict Canyon," and slammed down the phone.

The keys to all the cars were hanging on hooks. I found his key, went to his car – a beautiful metallic blue Mercedes 300SL – and opened it. The gull wing doors on both sides of the car opened up wide like a bird's wings. I mouthed a silent "wow," and got in.

When I started the car, I assumed the doors would automatically swing back down. But they did not. They stayed up. As I frantically tried to figure out where the switch was to bring the doors down, I was sweating profusely because he'd insisted that I get the car to him right away.

Finally, after about six or seven minutes, I threw caution to the wind, and started driving with the gull wing doors wide open. Like a bird running with its wings up, I drove through the back alleyways and side streets of Beverly Hills hoping I wouldn't hit anything, and no police officer would see me. I had to continually gauge the car's wingspan to make sure I wasn't going to hit anything on either side. In one particular alley a truck was sticking out, and it was going to be too close for comfort. I had to back my way out on to the street. It seemed like it took forever, but I was able to maneuver my way to Angelo Drive.

His house was at the very top of a large hill, like an eagle's nest. I drove up the winding road, gull wing doors still open. When I turned into his driveway, I saw him: He was standing on the balcony overlooking his courtyard, red-faced and scowling, with his arms crossed in front of him. He had watched me the entire way as I drove up Angelo Drive and I knew I was in for it.

He shouted down at me, "You idiot! Didn't someone show you how to close the doors?"

I said, "No, sir." I looked at my feet and stood there, waiting to be fired.

He turned away from the balcony, walked downstairs, and came to the side of the car.

"Come here," he said. He pointed to a switch on the inside of the glove compartment. "You see that switch? That's how you put the doors down."

"Thank you, sir," I said.

"Think you can handle that next time?"

"Yes, sir," I said. "Thank you, sir."

"Good. Now get back to the office. You'll have to walk because obviously I need the car." And he went in the house.

It was hot, I was wearing my dark gray suit and tie, and I was still sweating from the experience. I stood in the driveway, watched him go into the house, then turned and began the two-mile trek back to the office. I'm sure I looked ridiculous. After all, this was Los Angeles, where no one walked anywhere.

The whole way back I focused on the two most important words he'd said to me: "next time." With those words, "Think you can handle that *next time?*" I reasoned he had not fired me. There was still hope.

A couple of weeks later I had a rather unique encounter, up close and "sort of" personal, with Lew Wasserman. Lew was running the day-to-day operations of MCA at that time, working around the clock to drive the company's growth. He demanded that MCA agents have a more refined image than that of "flesh peddlers," and behave like he did – dress and act conservatively, and be available to clients 24 hours a day, seven days a week. It was grueling trying to follow his example.

However, his method worked. By the late 1950's, MCA was representing Bette Davis, James Stewart, Henry Fonda and seemingly every other major talent across film, television, radio, music and on Broadway. MCA had also become a diversified entertainment company that not only represented talent, but also produced content and created packaged deals that put their own clients in that content. In addition, with the major film studios unwilling to license their movies for television, Lew found a ready source in Paramount Pictures' pre-1948 library of 750 films, and he bought it for $50 million. That was in 1957, the year I started, and the deal brought in another lucrative revenue stream from television stations that were desperate to put programming on the air. That's just scratching the surface on the impact of Lew Wasserman.

In my first month at MCA, when the all-powerful and no-nonsense Lew Wassermann strode into the men's room, I was beyond intimidated. Rumor had it that he was so cold my pals in the mail room believed he could freeze an ice cream cone. I could not help myself. I took a peek and saw he wasn't really capable of freezing an ice cream cone...it was just the strategically placed ice in the men's room. I ran back and told my friends what I saw, and dispelled the myth; Mr. Wasserman was a human, after all.

Even though Jules Stein and Lew Wasserman weren't exactly the nurturing types, they did know they had to develop their people if their agency was going to be successful. That's one reason why they were so meticulous in their hiring and training practices. That's also why I was willing to put up with just about anything in order to get the experience I needed so I could have a successful career in entertainment.

Starting in the mailroom was the best thing that could have happened to me. Being in the number six position, I had to earn my way up the pecking order. In order for me to advance I had to outperform one of the five people ahead of me or one of them had to leave the agency or get promoted. I had all kinds of responsibilities, and I worked long hours, maybe 70 to 80 hours a week. There was no overtime pay in those days, but that was fine by me because I was learning something new every day. We often had screenings on Saturdays and Sundays, and I worked all days for those, too. I was in constant motion, and I got to know the agency, the industry, and the city very well.

It's funny how things come together. I could already navigate the west side of Los Angeles because of my experience making deliveries for Thrifty Drug Store in Beverly Hills. I never would have thought being a delivery boy would help me like it did, but it taught me a lesson I've tried to impart to others: every job has meaning, and you never know how it will benefit you. You owe it to your company, to your boss, and to yourself to do the best possible job you can.

In those days, part of being a good agent was wearing the right clothes and driving the right cars. That might sound superficial, but there was a reason for it. You didn't wear bright suits or bright ties or drive bright cars because you never wanted to draw attention away from your clients and toward yourself. Also, they were the artists and the clients, not you. You were a businessperson and should convey a sense of trust and accountability to them. They were talented people who often had to be emotionally vulnerable to do their jobs. You needed to be stable and grounded for them. What you wore and drove, and how you acted were all important parts of being an agent.

Eventually, as people moved on up from the other five positions at the mailroom who were ahead of me, I moved up, one position at a time, until I reached the number one spot. It took me about a year and a half to reach that point. Throughout the process, I got performance and salary reviews at regular intervals. When I finally left the mailroom, I was making $60 a week.

The next step was to be a floater, which was someone who filled in for agents' assistants when they were out sick or on vacation. That gave me a broader, yet more in-depth look at what was going on in each of the departments. For instance, in the literary and motion picture departments, I was able to read and comment on scripts, which gave me a better understanding of how a project moved from idea to script to casting to production to promotion. I loved it. During my time as a floater covering desks, I got to know the heads of the departments – Personal Appearance, Motion Picture, Acting, Television, Theater, Literary – and became friends with them. They remembered me from when I was interviewing there, and they could see I was making good progress.

Finally, I was promoted to be an assistant to Dale Sheets and Noel Rubaloff in the television department. I worked in an area that put actors, actresses, sportscasters, broadcast journalists and hosts/MCs in radio and television commercials, game shows, quiz shows, and audience participation shows. It was a fast-growing part of the agency and I found it all to be fascinating and exciting. I advanced quickly, becoming a full-fledged agent in a matter of months.

This was made possible, in part, because about 10 years earlier, in 1948, as television was beginning to be seen as a viable medium to some and a nuisance to the film studios, Jules Stein and Lew Wasserman embraced it, creating MCA TV. This unprecedented move meant MCA could produce films and television programs *and* represent the talent who worked on those films and programs. To make this a reality, Stein and Wasserman had to do two things.

First, they needed to overcome a major obstacle. SAG had stipulated that talent agencies were forbidden from producing TV shows and films. MCA needed a waiver. Fortunately, Lew Wasserman's good friend and client was Ronald Reagan, who had just been elected president of the Screen Actors Guild. With a waiver in hand from Reagan, MCA started producing TV shows.

Second, they needed a heavy hitter to run MCA TV; someone who knew both the production side of the business and the talent representation side. They had just the man in Mike Levee, a well-respected executive who had also started at the bottom and worked his way up. His first job in entertainment was at the age of 26, working for Fox as a prop man on Charles Dickens' *A Tale of Two Cities*, for which he earned $20 a week. Within three years he became president of United Artists. Three years after that he sold United Artists to Paramount Pictures, and joined Warner Bros. After three more years he left Warner Bros and founded his own one-man talent agency. Despite having no staff or organization he represented many of the era's most famous movie stars. So, with MCA free to produce content and represent talent, Mike Levee was a perfect fit to head the department.

Despite getting the waiver from Reagan, and hiring Levee, MCA didn't actually start producing content until 1950, when the company re-launched Revue Productions. Previously a live concert promoter that produced USO events during World War II, by 1956, Revue became the top supplier of television for all broadcast networks. Filming on the Republic Pictures lot in Studio City, Revue produced long-running hits such as *Leave it to Beaver*, the *Jack Benny Program*, *Alfred Hitchcock Presents*, *Wagon Train*, *Mike Hammer*, and many others.

MCA's voracious appetite for growth and power didn't stop there. In 1958, tired of paying to use the Republic Pictures lot, MCA bought the Universal Studios production facility from Universal Pictures for $11 million. Thus, Revue Productions had a new name – Revue Studios – and a new home. Looking to maximize its investment, MCA leased the space back to Universal for $2 million a year and freed up its stable of clients to star in Universal films.

By the end of the 1950s, MCA had become so dominant in so many areas of the entertainment industry people often referred to it as "the octopus." Two of the other leading agencies, William Morris and Famous Artists, believed MCA was a monopoly that was in violation of the Sherman-Clayton Antitrust Act, and should be broken up. They filed a lawsuit with the United States government, saying MCA either should stay in the talent agency business or stay in the motion picture and television production business. One or the other, but not both.

MCA fought it for years in court. Everyone at the agency was kept abreast of what was going on, and we knew that sooner or later, something was going to happen. Finally, in 1962, when MCA proposed a merger with Decca Records, which owned 89 percent of Universal Pictures, United States Attorney General Robert F. Kennedy had seen enough. In order to grant approval for the acquisition of Universal, Kennedy's Department of Justice told MCA to dissolve its talent agency. It was either that or get out of production.

It was a very simple decision on which direction to go. At that point, the gross dollar income from motion picture and television production was about $88 million, whereas the gross dollar revenue from the talent agency was about $8 million. The decision was final: MCA was staying in the motion picture and television production business.

The government said fine, but you cannot simply fire all of your employees. You have to offer every employee a position in motion picture and television production with Revue and Universal Pictures. This presented me and all of MCA's other agents with our own choice of staying and going into production or leaving and finding a job elsewhere. Several of us thought, well, there is a third option. We could open up our own talent agencies. Because the unions were in concert with the other big agencies and the government in breaking up MCA, all of the talent we represented were going to be without agents, cast to the wind.

Rather than view the breakup of MCA as a setback, I saw it as an opportunity. I reasoned MCA had been the king of the talent agency business, especially in radio and television commercials, MC/hosting, broadcast journalism – the areas in which we specialized. No agencies, except perhaps to a lesser degree, The William Morris Agency, had provided much in the way of competition. I thought, I could form my own talent agency, sign some of our best actors, and make a go of it.

Instead of opening a one-man shop, as Mike Levee had done when he formed his own agency 20 years earlier, I asked Noel Rubaloff to join me. Noel was eight years my senior, he knew a lot more about the business than I did, and he had taught me a great deal. I looked up to him, and I was proud to be associated with him.

When Noel and I went to the bank to open a bank account, and the bank manager asked, "What is the name of the company?" we realized we didn't have a name. We didn't even have a corporation. We didn't have a partnership. We did it all very quickly.

I said to Noel, "Abrams starts with A. If we call ourselves Abrams-Rubaloff & Associates, we'll be first on all the lists of agencies."

He said, "Great. Let's put your name first. We'll call it Abrams-Rubaloff & Associates."

"But we don't have any associates," I said.

"We can't just be two guys," he said. "That doesn't sound like much."

"You're right," I said. "Abrams-Rubaloff & Associates it is."

That's how my first talent agency business came into being. We leased space in a building owned by William Arthur Rush, the man who managed Roy Rogers and Dale Evans. The address was 357 North Canon Drive, around the corner from MCA's headquarters. I remember it vividly because in November of 1963, we were listening to the radio there in the office when John F. Kennedy was assassinated.

So many things were changing, and in a big way. The Kennedy administration had been called "Camelot," after the legendary realm of the mythical King Arthur, and with the snap of a finger, it was over. Gone went the glamorous "new frontier" of youthful idealism, sunny optimism, and unbridled energy. In came the harsh reality and cynicism of a new era. Still, the Kennedy administration had set in motion changes in our culture and attitudes that could never be turned back. As hard as it was, the country was prepared to go boldly into the future.

I, too, was prepared.

I was only 27 years old, but MCA had taught me how to become an agent. How to always be on the lookout for great talent. How to see actors, imagine what they might be capable of, and think of how I could give them better and more opportunities. I learned what it means to truly represent the best interests of the people I represented. How to teach them, coach them, and advise them on how to become stars if that's what they wanted to be. Just as often, I learned success means different things to different people, actors being no exception. Not every actor wants to be famous. Many just want to do good work, on high-quality projects, with other great talent. I considered myself privileged to have been a partner in their careers.

Similarly, at MCA I learned how an agency should operate. How to not be ostentatious. How to be assertive instead of aggressive and competitive without being cutthroat. Why it's important to be low key, under the radar, out of the limelight, behind the scenes, as far as publicizing or advertising. I have followed this philosophy throughout my career. In fact, whenever my agency made a major deal and it could be in the press, I always asked that we not be credited. It was drilled into my brain that as agents we succeeded when our clients were in the spotlight, not us.

Decades later, as the industry and business climate changed, I learned we needed to adapt so new people – clients and prospective employees – could know we existed and find us. To that end, after many, many years of flying under the radar, we created a website, hired an HR professional, and hired a public relations firm, then brought the function in-house. We began to run press releases and ads, and we searched for interviews and stories in which we could participate in the entertainment media outlets and any relevant news outlets. Since much of what I'm describing is about managing our image, we moved our New York office to 275 7th Avenue – one large floor with beautiful 360-degree views. This enabled talent and employees to see how large and diverse the company had become. It was impressive. In Los Angeles, we moved to the Red Building in the Pacific Design Center, which changed the look and feel of the agency from the old office to one that was more contemporary. In addition, we united the Los Angeles and New York offices, which brought more cohesiveness, and caused us to be taken more seriously.

My appreciation for all of these image-related developments was still a long way off. In the early days with Noel Rubaloff, decades before we created departments and professionalized functions, we were essentially a mom-and-pop shop. Or rather, since it was just Noel and me, a pop-and-pop shop.

Let's Do Launch

So, there we were in Los Angeles, armed with a bank account, a name for our business, office space, and everything we learned at MCA. There was only one thing left to do: sign some clients!

Chapter 9: Develop an Entrepreneurial Mindset

There's no business like show business
Like no business I know

—Irving Berlin
From *Annie Get Your Gun*

The days of working for one company, or in one career, are long gone. So is loyalty between companies and employees. Now, everyone is in perpetual startup mode. They're starting "side hustles" which is another way of saying they're starting business while they're still employed by others. And as the management guru and author, Tom Peters, wrote in Fast Company magazine back in 1997, "We are CEOs of our own companies: Me, Inc."

If you're starting a business, what skills do you need? Launching a new business is not for the faint of heart. Come to think of it, neither is launching a career, especially in entertainment. It requires belief, persistence, resourcefulness, salesmanship, agility, and a lot of hard work. Some would even say you have to be a little crazy.

This begs the question: what makes an entrepreneur successful? More than likely, an entrepreneur has to have a certain mindset. But can that even be developed? Every entrepreneur is unique and no path to success is the same, but all successful entrepreneurs share a specific skillset that allows them to solve problems, overcome obstacles, and thrive in their respective fields. Skills like the ability to control self-doubt, accountability, resiliency, the ability to adapt and overcome adversity, and a willingness to experiment and take chances are critical.

What did I, a 27-year-old relative neophyte, have going for me?

Although I didn't appreciate it at the time, my life's experiences had prepared me for the moment. I'd known what it meant to be poor, and to go without. I'd started and run a business, from the age of eight to the age of 13, selling newspapers. I'd been president of my high school class and a leader in my college fraternity. I'd been in charge of communications for one of the U.S. Army's largest bases. I ran a lawn mowing business. I was in charge of purchasing for a power lawn mower company. And I'd had my share of setbacks and disappointments. All of this and more prepared me for what I set out to do.

But the truth is, if MCA hadn't been forced to break up, I may have stayed there for the rest of my career. I'd become a talent agent at the world's most successful agency, which is all I ever wanted. I was helping talented people build their careers. In the process, I was seeing as many films, plays, musicals, ballets and concerts as my heart desired. And my heart desired a lot.

But things changed. And like it or not, I was now an entrepreneur.

When we started Abrams-Rubaloff & Associates, we stuck to what we knew best. We signed radio and television personalities, newscasters, sportscasters, disc jockeys, hosts and MCs and we got them work on game shows, quiz shows and audience participation shows, and in commercials, on and off camera. That was our specialty, and it was a good niche for us because that part of the entertainment industry was still emerging. Other talent agencies weren't interested in that unglamorous side of the business, but we knew there was a lot of opportunity in it. At the same time, it was like the wild west – untamed, much like social media is today.

We started and grew that business on our own. We built and nurtured relationships with people who could hire our talent. Slowly, we added staff, training young people in the way we'd been trained at MCA. Minus the yelling and insults, of course. We didn't have much competition, which helped. There were a couple of small agencies, and

William Morris had a couple of agents who were half-heartedly doing what we were doing. But we committed to this area, and we thrived.

However, it was much tougher than being at a large corporation which had a long history of success. The name of MCA would open doors anywhere. People would return our telephone calls, open our mail, and take our meetings. They would respond to us, without fail. Being on our own was difficult, and we had to forge relationships, often starting from scratch. We used whatever we could in the way of contacts. In today's parlance, we followed the maxim, "fake it till you make it."

If an important client or buyer or producer or casting director called us, we would try to meet them in person. If they were in Los Angeles, we'd get together for coffee, invite them out to lunch, have a drink with them, go by their office and get to know them. That was the nature of the agency business. You could not be a shrinking violet and survive. You had to put yourself out there and forget about being rejected.

Because we specialized in what we were doing — we were not motion picture, television, or theatrical agents — we became in-demand and built up a good reputation within the space of a year or two years.

Some rifts between us became apparent early on. To begin with, Noel never worked in a mailroom. Let alone, MCA's mailroom. Consequently, he did not have the much sought-after "MCA MBA" that gave him the necessary training. He had been a syndicated film and television salesman for United Television Programs (UTP). When MCA acquired UTP, Noel came with the deal.

I was far more ambitious and aggressive and driven than Noel was. I was the one who wanted to travel around the country to different markets, like Chicago and New York, where the big advertising agencies were located. Noel thought Los Angeles was big enough, and he saw no need to go anywhere else. Particularly New York, which he hated. I wanted to sell talent on camera and off camera, in as many markets as I could. The ultimate, as far as I was concerned, was to represent the top spokespersons on behalf of products and services all over the country.

In 1966, after about three years of going back and forth between Los Angeles and New York, making deals for our clients with the biggest advertising agencies on Madison Avenue, I took a big risk, and opened a New York office. It was a substantial investment in time and money. First of all, talent agency commissions were regulated by the federal and state governments. This meant you had to pay a fee to be licensed by the State Labor Commissioners of New York and California. You also had to pay to be franchised by the guilds or the unions in order to represent the members, their actors. Also, the state and federal agencies that had jurisdiction over our line of work put a cap on what we could charge – a straight 10 percent commission. As a matter of fact, that's how talent agents earned the nickname the "ten percenters."

In addition to those investments, I had to find office space. A friend of mine, Carl Eastman, a top voiceover agent in New York with whom I shared clients, gave me space in his home, a beautiful brownstone, in exchange for marketing his clients to the advertising agencies.

One of Carl's clients, whom I eventually inherited, was a terrific character actor named Mason Adams, the voice of Smucker's jams and jellies. If you heard the line, "With a name like Smucker's, it has to be good" you heard Mason. Mason received three Emmy nominations for Best Supporting Actor for his work on the long-running television show, *Lou Grant*. He also acted in plays by his fellow Brooklynite and University of Michigan classmate, Arthur Miller. To top it off, Mason's birth name was Mason Abrams. I have no idea if we were related, but his wonderful last name must explain his talent and good looks.

In my case, I was determined, working day and night, to build the New York office, and the business took off. Within a few short months I moved out of Carl Eastman's home and leased some legitimate office space. Considering how expensive New York City commercial real estate was, even then, that's quite a success story.

Noel didn't see it that way. I would come to Los Angeles four or five times a year, each time reporting greater and greater growth from New York. Noel didn't care. He wanted to keep the business small. I wanted the business to grow, to expand. He did not see why it couldn't be just the two of us and one assistant back in Los Angeles. Try as I might, I couldn't get him to see beyond that. We had many tense discussions about this, and big cracks in our relationship were beginning to form.

At the same time, in the back of my mind, I'd always been curious to see if we could diversify beyond commercials and into representing actors and actresses for work in film and television and theatre. I wasn't content to expand geographically; I wanted us to get into entirely new areas of representation. I mean, I was in New York City, which was filled with fantastic actors!

It frustrated me to no end to be representing artists – actors and actresses I had discovered – who wanted to use commercials to supplement their serious acting careers, and not be able to do anything for them beyond that. They had studied acting. They had gone to NYU and Yale and RADA. They were still taking classes with Lee Strasberg and Stella Adler and HB Studio and the Neighborhood Playhouse, where, incidentally, Mason Adams taught for several years. These professionals wanted to act in film and television and on stage in legitimate theater. And so, I wanted to move us into that area as well. After all, I had found many actors and actresses, and gotten them a lot of work in commercials who went on to become famous. I had brought these actors and actresses into prominence, given them visibility, and elevated their profiles. Most of all, I helped them earn a good living practicing their art in an expensive city. They knew it, and they were grateful for all I had done for them. However, when producers or casting directors or networks wanted to hire them as professional actors and actresses, they had other agents for that. We weren't in that part of the business. As a result, we were on the outside looking in.

I used to have big fights with Noel about this. He felt it was a much tougher business model to try to represent actors for all of their income, for their whole career. He feared they would be disloyal to us and jump to other agencies, a not unfounded concern. He reasoned the business we were in was a small niche area we could control. We were specialists, and we were the best, and that was good enough for him.

In addition, like many entrepreneurs, I had the added pressure of being a husband and father. It's difficult to juggle the demands of starting and running a business, traveling around the country, and keeping relationships. It's tough for actors and actresses, too. For anyone, really. And I was having a hard time with it.

In 1962, I married a woman named Roslyn Ritter, whom I met on her very first day working at MCA. Roz was from New York and had moved to Los Angeles with her family a couple of years earlier. She was 20 years old, beautiful, creative and energetic, and I fell in love the moment I set eyes on her.

Roz would be the first to tell you she was raised by her parents to get married. That's how it was for most women in those days. Although it was 1962, the culture of the country was still in the prior decade. Unfortunately, that left women few career options: be a teacher, nurse or secretary. And all of those options came in third behind being a wife and mother.

In our first seven years, Roz and I had three sons: Tony, Jonathan, and Nicolas. We lived in West Los Angeles, and I worked hard at juggling my business and family responsibilities. There are many pictures of me with the kids during those years. I loved them dearly, and I loved my life with my family and my work, and you can see that in the photos. What you can't see is what was going on in my head. Thoughts of "I have to sign clients, I have to make deals, I have to grow the business" were continuous. It pains me to think that sometimes, even though I was physically present, I may not have been all the way there emotionally. You could say I was a product of the era in which I was raised. But that doesn't make it easier to also consider the possibility that my business and my clients were my first love, and if the time I spent working versus being a husband and father is indicative of where my priorities lay during this time period, my family came in second. If you know me now, and you know the person I've become, you know how much that hurts me. What hurts me more is that it hurt my family.

In early 1963, before we started having kids, Roz's father took us on a trip to New York City. It was my first time there, and my eyes were wide open, as was my mind. With George Gershwin's *Rhapsody in Blue* as the soundtrack playing in my head during that trip, my love affair with New York City began to take shape. This was a city of great music, and theatre, and art, and ballet, and literature, and yes, the world's biggest advertising agencies. The possibilities for life and work were endless, and I silently started dreaming about how I could get to New York. I simply had to be there.

Three years later, it happened. When I opened the New York office in 1966, Roz and the kids came with me. We rented a beautiful place on 65th Street and York Avenue with a clear view of the East River. It was actually three apartments that had been combined into one, and although I didn't know it when I signed the lease, Johnny Carson had just moved out. It may sound glamorous to be living in the apartment formerly occupied by "The King of Late Night." It was most assuredly not.

There's a reason why people say if you can make it in New York, you can make it anywhere. New York in those days was tough for many reasons. I was opening up my own little business there, and since Noel didn't support the move, I was professionally by myself. It was the first time I had lived in New York, and we had a brutal winter.

From an environmental standpoint, New York City had the worst air pollution among big cities in the United States. Multiple power plants burned coal and heavy grades of oil, which belched noxious fumes into the air. The smog was so bad it filled the air with damaging levels of several toxic pollutants including carbon monoxide and sulfur dioxide. There were many days when our view of the East River was obscured by a yellow haze of smog which you could wipe with a rag. Consequently, the city declared an environmental disaster and advised people with respiratory or heart conditions to remain indoors. The city also shut down nearly 20,000 garbage incinerators that were causing flakes of burned garbage to fall like snow.

At first, New York City officials denied that the smog was anything more than a nuisance and not a public health emergency. However, a study published in December 1966 estimated that the smog had caused 10 percent of the city's citizens to develop severe health problems, such as burning and irritated eyes, hacking coughs, and respiratory illnesses like pulmonary emphysema and chronic bronchitis.

Roz and our youngest son, Jonathan, became very ill with bronchitis. It was extremely difficult because I was all by myself in the office during the day and trying to take care of my family at the same time. We soldiered on until we'd had enough. Finally, Roz took the children to Los Angeles and the warm weather so they could get back to good health before returning to New York.

The New York office grew quickly. By 1968, I had hired and trained a few people into our business including Peter Beilin and Steve

Carbone, both of whom went on to start their own businesses and have successful entertainment careers. Things were going well until I was forced to handle a situation in Los Angeles. Herb Tannen, a fellow I had trained who was heading our voice department in Los Angeles, left the company in 1968 to open his own shop. This left us with a big hole in our business. Although Noel was in the Los Angeles office he confined himself to our emcee and hosting arena, and I was the only one who knew our voice business. That meant I had to cut my New York stay short – my plan had been to be there for about seven years – and go back to Los Angeles, where I would rebuild our voice department.

Once again, I packed up the family and moved across the country. This time, to our new home in the Brentwood section of Los Angeles. My New York staff continued to run the office there, and I went back and forth just as I had before. My plan was to stay in Los Angeles until I felt I had trained people sufficiently, which I thought might take about three or four years, and then move back to New York.

For her part, Roz had become a good corporate wife and a great mother, but she was not feeling fulfilled in her life. We began to grow apart. We had a big, beautiful home and a live-in nanny, and although Roz liked the house well enough, as a stay-at-home mom she felt isolated. She met some, in her words, "hippie parents" in another neighborhood, and wanted to move there. I was happy with our life right where we were. She wanted to drive up and down the coast in one of those iconic Volkswagen buses. Instead, when our son, Nicolas, was born in 1969, I bought a "more sensible" Mercury station wagon she could use to cart around the kids.

With the political and societal unrest of the 1960s in full bloom, and a massive culture change underway, I think it's safe to say Roz was experiencing an awakening of spirit not unlike much of the rest of the country. At the same time, I was hunkering down, an entrepreneur in a conservative suit and tie, trying to grow a business.

In April of 1968, the great civil rights leader, Martin Luther King, Jr., was assassinated. While running for president just two months later, Robert F. Kennedy was assassinated in Los Angeles. Vietnam protests were in the streets. The Chicago Democratic convention erupted in violence. Richard Nixon won the presidency.

Woodstock was upon us in 1969, and we were the first country to put a man on the moon. It was an incredible time, but it was hard to even catch a breath.

To escape it all we bought a home in Lake Tahoe. Crisp, clean air. Gorgeous scenery. Beautiful blue water. Skiing and swimming on the same day. It was heaven on earth. It pains me to see the area currently being threatened by massive wildfires.

Most of the people there were from San Francisco, and Roz loved it. She met other young, smart, and interesting women, and made many good friends. Consequently, she began to spend more and more time there. Who could blame her? After all, it was paradise.

Then, one day in 1971, Roz went to dinner at the home of one of her new friends, met a man who happened to be there that evening, and fell for him. They entered into a romantic relationship, and the end of our marriage had begun.

Roz and I divorced in 1972, and she took the kids to live in a teepee near Santa Cruz.

I'm not being snide or sarcastic in saying that; they really did live in a canvas teepee.

As shocking as it was to me, in the '60s and '70s it was common for many anti-war protesters, environmentalists and social change activists to live together in "intentional communities" of cabins and teepees in Northern California. For instance, in the Santa Cruz Mountains alone, quite a few people lived in a cluster of communes

Tony
credit: Maya Myers

with names such as Struggle Mountain, Rancho Diablo, Earth Ranch and most famously, The Land. About 10 years before it ended in 1977 with an eviction notice, bulldozers and arrests for the men and women who refused to leave it, The Land was founded by the folk singer Joan Baez as the Institute for the Study of Non-Violence, which would later become part of the Resource Center for Non-Violence.

Jonathan
credit: Maya Myers

Roz and our boys lived in one of these communities, though I'm not sure which one.

My son Tony recently said how much of a shock it was to move from our beautiful home in Los Angeles to the teepee. He chuckles at it now, and today he can tell a funny, however rueful, story about it. But I know it was heartbreaking for all of us, Roz included.

Recently, Tony recalled how sad and sweet it was that I tried to learn guitar and sing folk songs so I could hang on to Roz. The thought of me, a tanned salesman in a tailored suit, trying to be Bob Dylan, a pale counterculture hero in hippie garb, feebly playing guitar and warbling "Blowin' in the Wind" in our backyard, is comical now. And yes, sad, even pathetic. But I suppose it was also naively endearing. It aptly illustrates how desperately I wanted to keep our family together. It was to no avail, however, because Roz wanted out. Not just because she met another man, but because she was becoming a different person – perhaps uncovering her true self – who wanted more from her life.

After our divorce, we didn't talk much for quite a few years, which was especially hard on the kids. Making matters worse, Roz remained friends with Noel Rubaloff as my relationship with him went sour. With my partnership with Noel headed for the rocks and my marriage to Roz already crashed, I was stranded and alone.

Nicolas
credit: Maya Myers

69

Such is the life of an entrepreneur. Well, at least this entrepreneur. So, too is the life of actors, actresses, writers, directors and anyone else in the entertainment industry. There are so many competing priorities it is tough to keep it all straight. To do the right thing. To be ethical, and to make choices that are good for everyone and not just you. You have to somehow be selfish and generous at the same time, and it's not easy. For those who decide to work in this industry I say beware, and congratulations. Beware, because there are countless traps and betrayals and soul-crushing disappointments. Congratulations, because there is more joy and satisfaction than you could ever possibly imagine.

Today, I have good relationships with all the kids I had with Roz, who is a terrific mother and became a wonderful artist. Tony is a screen writer and director, Jonathan is a musician and stay-at-home dad, and Nicolas is a chef who now owns a business called Ethel's Delicatessen which is named after his grandmother. The bagels are delicious!

Chapter 10: When Opportunities Knock, Answer Them

Open the gates and seize the day
Don't be afraid and don't delay

—Alan Mencken and Jack Feldman
From *Newsies*

One spring day in 1969, I had one of those "only in New York" experiences.

I was with Roz and the kids in Central Park, having a picnic. We were sitting on a blanket with Nicolas, our newborn, with lunch spread out around us, while Tony and Jonathan were playing with a ball nearby. When the ball got loose and bounced over to a group of young women sitting about 30 yards away, Tony ran after it. The women looked harmless enough, but we still didn't want our seven-year-old son casually approaching a group of strangers, especially in Central Park, on that day.

You see, a combination peace rally and "be-in" – short for human being – was taking place in the Sheep Meadow on the other side of the park. About 20,000 hippies, Vietnam War protesters, activists, and artists of all kinds were in the park that day agitating for peace. Ironically, unlike peace rallies and be-ins of prior years, which featured musicians and crowds of people mostly getting high, listening to music and relaxing, this event was anything but peaceful. Angry demonstrators were throwing rocks at the police, shouting and shoving,

Jaclyn Smith

and setting enormous bonfires. With the ground burned and trampled it looked like the scene of a battle.

And our little Tony was running toward it.

Before I could retrieve Tony, one of the young women was escorting him, and the ball, back to us. She didn't so much walk as she did glide across the space between us. The closer she got the more luminous and graceful she became. When she finally reached us, she smiled and said, in a thick and sweet southern accent, "I believe this handsome young man belongs to you?"

It was Jaclyn Smith. She must have been in her early 20s, and she was studying at American Ballet Theatre. She and her friends had gone to Central Park to audition for a show starring Andy Williams and William Shatner. They needed dancers and Jaclyn and her friends were all students eager for a job. They were staying at the Barbizon Hotel on East 63rd street, not far from where we lived on 65th.

I knew all of this because I struck up a conversation with her as I walked her back to her group. Being an opportunistic agent with an eye for talent, I asked her if she had ever acted or done any commercial work, either in print or on television. She said she had studied drama at Trinity University where she was in "Bye Bye Birdie," "West Side Story," and "Gentlemen Prefer Blondes." But she left after a year to pursue her dream of being a dancer in New York.

I said her classic beauty made her a natural for television cameras, and I gave her my card. I'd never seen anyone as beautiful as her, and I could imagine her image and voice gracing all manner of ads and products, especially those in the beauty category.

After we agreed that I would represent her, I sent Jaclyn to a vocal coach to try to iron out her southern accent. She studied acting with legendary teachers such as Herbert Berghof, and Robert Modica. And of course, she continued to dance. She worked hard at her craft. In addition to the training, which she was eager to get, she wanted to learn how, in her words, "to do things right, to be a serious professional, to have a champion to advise her and advocate for her."

Her hard work paid off for both of us. Before long, Jaclyn was beamed into American homes as "The Breck Girl" for Gold Formula Breck. She starred in their commercials, on their packaging, on billboards, and in print ads, all of which I handled and looked after.

Gold Formula Breck was with BBDO Advertising at the time. I made a one-year deal with their creative director, Jim Jordan, on Jaclyn's behalf. Although Jaclyn's work had been a big hit and had greatly benefitted Gold Formula Breck, Breck Shampoo, Breck Hair Coloring and their other brands, at the end of the year Jim and BBDO didn't renew her contract.

We were disappointed, but we knew Jaclyn was going places. And I knew I was going to help her get there.

I did some digging and learned Alberto Balsam was introducing a new shampoo and the James Neal Harvey advertising agency was going to handle the campaign. I knew Jim Harvey, and I took Jaclyn over to meet with him. She was well-known from her work with Breck, and he flipped over her. I wasn't surprised; she had that effect on people. Even more so when you met her in person. The product was Wella Balsam, and Jim wrote the opening television spot himself. I remember Jaclyn came on camera and said, "I'm Jaclyn Smith and I've switched to Wella Balsam Shampoo. I'm really glad I did. Because. . ." and she went on to talk about the product's attributes. It was a big hit. Here was a new shampoo taking on Breck, the more established competitor, and they were using the former Breck spokesperson to do it.

Jaclyn's star was officially launched. She did campaigns for English Leather, Max Factor and countless other beauty and self-care products. She launched her own fragrance, *California*, with Max Factor. And that was just the start of her rise to superstardom.

Soon, Hollywood beckoned, and she appeared in popular TV series such as *McCloud*, *The Rookies* and *Switch*. In 1976, Aaron Spelling called me and cast Jaclyn as Kelly Garrett on *Charlie's Angels*. She was the only actor to continue with the series for its five-year network run. Following *Charlie's Angels*, Jaclyn earned a Golden Globe nomination for her critically acclaimed portrayal of the legendary first lady in *Jacqueline Bouvier Kennedy*, one of the most highly rated telefilms of all time. Frequently called the "Queen of Mini-Series," Jaclyn starred in such well received mini-series and films as *Rage of Angels*, *George Washington*, *Rage of Angels: The Story Continues*, *The Bourne Identity*, *Family Album*, and *Florence Nightingale*.

In 1985, Jaclyn entered the business world with the introduction of her collection of women's apparel and accessories for Kmart stores. She pioneered the concept of celebrities developing their own brands rather than merely endorsing others. Since that time more than 100 million women have purchased clothing or accessories bearing her name. Awareness of the Jaclyn Smith brand by women 35-60 years of age is currently higher than 80 percent, making her one of the best recognized people in America. Industry authority *Woman's Wear Daily reported* that the signature Jaclyn Smith line once had the highest consumer awareness of any private label apparel brand in the country.

With her sincere desire to help consumers attain beautiful home décor at an affordable price, Jaclyn began working with one of the world's largest home textile wholesalers, Trend/Fabricut on an exclusive fabric and trimming program in 2007.

In 2008, Jaclyn launched her new line of bed and bath decor at Kmart and has since introduced outdoor living, home furnishings and seasonal items. The items bearing her name reflect many of the inspiring details and exceptional design of furnishings and accessories found in her personal collection and her exceptional eye for detail translates effortlessly to timeless designs.

Along with her longtime friend and famed celebrity hair stylist, José Eber, Jaclyn also created a new collection of hair fashions, STYLE by Jaclyn Smith in partnership with Paula Young which also launched in 2008.

In 2010, Jaclyn collaborated with her husband, Dr. Brad Allen, a renowned medical researcher, to develop a family of luxurious cleansers and moisturizers, and protective skin care products to work with her straightforward daily regimen – and to work in perfect concert with each other.

And acting has not taken a backseat as Jaclyn has appeared in more than 40 television episodes since 2010.

According to market research, Jaclyn ranks in the top quartile of celebrity personas, on level with Ralph Lauren and Walt Disney. Jaclyn scores equally high with both men and women, has essentially no negatives, and is known not only for beauty, elegance and class, but is trustworthy and someone people aspire to be.

You may wonder why I'm spending so much time talking about Jaclyn Smith.

First, Jaclyn Smith is a perfect example of someone who put in the work to be ready when opportunity knocked. When it did, in the form of my initial conversation with her in Central Park, she grabbed it, taking the momentum she gained in commercials and print advertising and riding it to Hollywood and beyond.

Once the door cracked open ever so slightly, she didn't wait for someone to open it the rest of the way; she kicked it in, politely, of course. When she realized she could capitalize on her fame by becoming a businesswoman, she didn't wait and hope that someone would think like she did; she made it happen herself. Despite all her success, today she will tell you that her most important accomplishments are her two children.

The point is you don't have to be one-dimensional in your life. You're not just an actor, actress, writer, producer, director, dancer, singer, musician, agent or businessperson. You're whatever you want to be. You're not waiting for opportunity. You're preparing for it and creating it.

I'm talking about Jaclyn Smith for another reason: My professional relationship with her was largely finished when she started working on *Charlie's Angels*. As happy as I am for all her incredible success as an artist and a businesswoman, and as grateful as I am for our continued friendship through all of these years, I regret I was not able to actively participate in her professional success in Hollywood.

When opportunity knocked, I couldn't answer. Because although I wanted us to grow, and the growth was there for the taking, Noel Rubaloff wanted us to stay small. For example, because Noel didn't want us to be in the theatrical business, when Jaclyn went to Hollywood, I had to send her to another agent and agency in Los Angeles—Jimmy Cota, at the Artists Agency. It wasn't more than three or four months after I introduced them that they were representing her exclusively in the theatrical arena.

Imagine how that felt. It was 1975 or 1976, and Aaron Spelling was casting a new television pilot called *Charlie's Angels*. He said to his casting director, "Get me the girl who speaks for Breck." Because of my relationship with Jaclyn, the call came to me. But I couldn't do anything with it because I wasn't in that business. I referred the call to Jimmy, and that was Jaclyn's beginning in Hollywood.

There were numerous incidents of this happening. For instance, it was frustrating to have my client Susan Blakely leave me in 1976 to star in nearly 100 films and television shows, including *The Towering Inferno* and *Rich Man, Poor Man*—after I'd helped her get started with Revlon. Likewise with Veronica Hamel, who went on to do *Hill Street Blues*, *Third Watch*, *Lost*, and dozens of other theatrical projects; and Lauren Hutton, who did *The Gambler*, *American Gigolo*, and more. There are so many more it pains me to think of it.

Finally, I figured out a path through this stalemate with Noel – I'd represent actors and actresses in soap operas.

Most of the motion picture and network television work was in Los Angeles. As much as I wanted to get into that business, I was in New York, so I decided to hold off on pursuing it—for the time being. New York, on the other hand, was where most of the soap operas were being produced, and where serious theatre was happening. Also, it was a natural extension from my commercial work because soap operas were closely allied with Procter & Gamble, who was the biggest producer of television commercials, and they also owned and created soap operas.

This meant that the same type of talent Procter & Gamble was buying for soap operas like *As the World Turns*, *The Edge of Night*, *Guiding Light*, *Search for Tomorrow* and *Another World* were the same type of people I sold commercially—good-looking actors and actresses, leads, supporting actors, and everyone from the glamorous to the more relatable "guy on the street." It was an easy transition for me to move from representing the talent commercially to selling them in soap operas, and vice versa.

Susan Lucci was one of my first soap opera clients. She had been playing the wildly popular Erica Kane on the half-hour *All My Children* since its debut in 1970, and she was about four years into the show before I started representing her. When ABC expanded the show to one hour, I was able to leverage Susan's popularity and that of the show and successfully renegotiate her contract, getting her much more favorable terms. *TV Guide* called her "Daytime's Leading Lady," and the *New York Times* and *Los Angeles Times* cited her as the highest-paid actor in daytime television. She starred on the show for all 41 years of its run, winning an Emmy Award in 1999.

With Susan's appearance in advertising campaigns for Riunite wine and Close-Up toothpaste, I was also able to begin executing my strategy of getting soap actors and actresses work in television commercials. This was a game-changer for me as I then signed several of Susan's *All My Children* colleagues including Ruth Warrick, Julia Barr, Richard Van Vleet, Candice Earley, Mary Fickett, Pippa Pearthree and many others.

Building on my *All My Children* success, I began representing talent on *As the World Turns*, *The Edge of Night*, *One Life to Live*, and other New York-based shows. One such person was the Emmy-winning actress Robin Strasser, who moved from NBC's *The Secret Storm* and *Another World* to ABC's *All My Children* and *One Life to Live*. A native New Yorker, Robin was a graduate of the Yale School of Drama and a founding member of the American Conservatory Theatre in San Francisco. That's some serious acting training.

My foray into the world of New York theatre was also taking hold. After seeing the legendary actor Lee J. Cobb in a play in New York – Lee had been the original Willy Loman years earlier in Arthur Miller's *Death of a Salesman* – I talked my way past the ushers and went backstage to see if I could meet him. I have to admit that took a lot of guts. Lee J. Cobb was a titan of the stage and screen. He was known for his deep husky voice, angry scowl and bulky broad-shouldered frame and the thought of talking with him was intimidating.

I found his dressing room and knocked on the door.

"What is it?" he yelled from behind the closed door.

"Mr. Cobb, my name is Harry Abrams, and I. . ."

"Who?"

"Harry Abrams, sir. I'd like to talk with you for a minute."

The door cracked open, and there he was.

"Whadd'ya want?" he said.

"Mr. Cobb, I am a commercial talent agent. . .I have my own talent agency here in New York, and I represent actors for television and radio commercials. I know you're a highly trained classical actor but I'm wondering if you would ever consider lending your voice talents to a commercial."

He looked at me, blankly.

"It may seem rather crass of me to say this, Mr. Cobb. In fact, I'm sure it is. But I'd just like to say that you can make an awful lot of money for just a little bit of work."

His face softened, and he grinned.

"Harry, my boy, I may have lofty principles, but I can be bought."

That's how I came to represent the great Lee. J. Cobb, for whom I negotiated a three-year deal to do radio and television commercial voice overs for Pan Am. Years later, when I was speaking with him at his home in California, he told me he made more money doing those commercials than he'd ever made in his theatrical career. He said it changed his life. This was gratifying to me, and it wouldn't have happened unless I'd gone to the theatre in New York City.

Lee J. Cobb

In another instance, I saw *A Chorus Line* Off-Broadway at the Public Theatre in 1975, and then again when it was moved to the Shubert Theatre on Broadway. It was there that I saw someone who would become another client of mine, the beautiful and talented Kelly Bishop, who won the Tony Award for playing Sheila in *A Chorus Line*.

Kelly was a trained ballet dancer and she moved like one, with an uncommon combination of strength and sensuality and silkiness. When she sang *At the Ballet* I was completely enthralled, and I knew I had to meet her. She was initially represented by another agency for her work in film and television, so we signed her for commercial work. When I spoke with her, Kelly told me how an agent at her other agency – the one who represented her for film and television – told her, "It's a shame you didn't get the "Tits and Ass" song." She said that's when she knew she had the wrong agent. Plus, he wasn't getting her any work. I was struck by how she said she wanted to be a straight actor instead of a dancer. How she wanted to be a working actor, not a star. And this was after winning the Tony! Her philosophy and values appealed to me greatly and fit my idea of what success was. It was about the work; about the sheer love of it and commitment to it and the desire to do whatever it took to do it and do it well.

I went to see Kelly as often as I could whenever she was on a set, including when she did *Dirty Dancing* and *Gilmore Girls*. I wasn't the only one who clicked with Kelly; all our agents did. Over time we represented Kelly for all her work – regional theatre, feature films, television guest spots, pilots, soap operas, commercials. You name it.

David Strathairn

She was still with our agency when I retired, and we remain good friends to this day.

I could name a lot of actors I found and represented in New York theatre. But I'll call out just one more: David Strathairn. David was a soft-spoken and intense actor who took his craft seriously. He had, and has, great integrity, and as such, he would only appear in parts about which he felt strongly. When he confided to a friend that those kinds of parts were not coming his way quickly enough, and he thought he might need an agent to help him find more work like that, his friend suggested he talk with me.

David made an appointment to come see me. I took him to lunch, and we got to know each other over the course of two or three hours. Talking about it now, David said it didn't even feel like we were discussing business, and that I belied the notion he had of slick, fast-talking agents who tout their connections and promise the world while delivering nothing. He recalls how I asked him a lot of questions to understand his philosophy about work and life, and how I took the time to find out who he was and what he really wanted to do. As was my custom, I did a lot more listening than talking, and I filled a yellow legal pad with notes from what I heard. Also, David remembers how I never tried to get him to sign with me in that lunch, and that the only thing I asked of him was where he was performing next so I could come see his work.

Finally, I saw David in an obscure off-off Broadway play, advised him to continue to work in the theatre, and eventually moved him to Broadway. As he said when we met, he only wanted to do theatre. However, his college classmate, John Sayles, was directing an indie film he'd written, *The Return of the Secaucus 7*, and cast David in the film. Thereafter, David only wanted to play character roles on stage and in feature films. It was only after many years of me asking him to consider television—since he could earn a lot more money and get wider exposure—that he began starring in television and films.

Since we first met, David has performed in a prolific mix of huge box-office movies and more independent films. He has earned every accolade he's received, and I believe he has his integrity, not to mention his talent and hard work, to thank for it. Again, he is exactly the kind of person with whom I want to be associated, and by whom others should be inspired.

Despite the proven success of Abrams-Rubaloff & Associates in New York, not only in the commercial arena but in soap operas and legitimate theatre, Noel still didn't agree with my strategy of expanding into motion pictures and network television in Hollywood. He didn't mind taking the money; he owned half our stock, and I owned the other. But he didn't want the responsibility, and he didn't want any of our other agents in Los Angeles to be "distracted" by this. He preferred to stay in the radio and television commercial world, and deal with MCs, hosts, and broadcast journalists, which was our specialty and our niche, and with which we had been successful in Los Angeles and New York.

But my years in New York affected me because I could see what was possible. There were highly trained actors and actresses in New York who were doing great theatre, and I saw a lot of their performances. I even put them in many of those shows. The theatre was notoriously underpaying, and I helped them a great deal by getting them work on soap operas and in television and radio commercials. I knew, sooner or later, they would want to be in films and on prime-time television. And if we weren't there for them, we would be on the outside looking in.

After years of flying back and forth, and having heated arguments over our future, I'd had enough. I told Noel I was going to move back to Los Angeles and run this area of the business myself. I said I had people I had trained who could look after the actors and actresses in New York. And although I would continue to keep an eye on New York, I was going to go all out to capitalize on the opportunity in Los Angeles. He didn't like that at all. And much to his dismay, I moved back anyway.

The person I left in charge of the New York office was Don Buchwald, who had been in the agency business before joining our company, but not in the arena of commercials or broadcast journalism where I'd built my career. He was some years my junior, and over the course of about four or five years I taught him the business. He was very, very good at it and I had complete confidence in him. In fact, Don had become like a brother to me.

In the months leading up to my move back to Los Angeles, I sometimes brought Don with me so he and Noel could get to know each other a bit. Don was bringing in a lot of business and was becoming very important to the company. Because of this, I wanted to eventually give him a financial participation in the New York office and an equity position as well. Not a huge position, but enough to recognize his contributions and let him know how important he was to our future. Of course, Don wanted the same thing and felt he deserved it because he would be running the New York office.

A few days before I left for Los Angeles, Don and I had a long dinner at the Friars Club in New York City. I told him Noel and I had been in business together for 14 or 15 years at this point, and despite my best efforts to persuade him to go in the direction I thought was best for the company, it wasn't working. I said I'd try one more time to convince Noel to give Don equity, but if he refused, I'd tell Noel we should go our separate ways. Finally, I'd tell Noel that Don and I share the same philosophy about the business, and we're going to become partners in our own company.

Don was thrilled I was throwing down the gauntlet and making this commitment to him. We shook hands to seal the deal.

The next day, in our Los Angeles office, I once again made my pitch to Noel. Noel, of course, strongly disagreed. He didn't want to part with any of his equity position and said, "Well, if you want to give him an equity position, give him part of your 50 percent ownership in the company. Not mine."

After a few weeks of me being in Los Angeles and pursuing this new area of the business, Noel was barely tolerating my presence. I never thought it would get to this point, but we were arguing so much it became difficult for us to work together. Something – or someone – was bound to crack.

Chapter 11: Even Hollywood
Can Get Ugly

Just like Julius Caesar
Was betrayed by Brutus
Who'd think an accountant
Would turn out to be my Judas!
I'm so dismayed
Is this how I'm repaid?
To be... Betrayed!

—Mel Brooks
From *The Producers*

Los Angeles, and Hollywood in particular, is known for being the land of beautiful people. From a purely physical perspective, whether it's because of plastic surgery or personal trainers, it's true. At the same time, I'm reminded of something the writer Dorothy Parker said, "Beauty is only skin deep, but ugly goes clean to the bone."

I experienced this firsthand when Noel Rubaloff met me at the front door to our office in Los Angeles on a Saturday morning, handed me a piece of paper, and said he was calling a meeting of our board of directors in a couple of hours. When I asked him for the agenda he said, "I'd just like to have a meeting with the board of directors. The three of us will sit down and we will talk about the future of the company."

The three of us he was referring to were himself, Dorothy Stewart and me. I had hired Dorothy to be our bookkeeper many years earlier, and she was a wonderful, trustworthy woman, very ethical and dedicated to the company. She did her job well and we rewarded her with a seat on our board. I considered her a friend as well as a colleague. However, during the years I had been in New York, obviously I wasn't interacting with her as much as Noel, who saw her every day. As a result, Dorothy and Noel had become close, from a professional standpoint, which is entirely understandable.

What happened at that meeting was not.

As soon as we sat down in the boardroom Noel dispensed with the usual pleasantries, called the meeting to order, and said he and Dorothy had voted to terminate my services at Abrams-Rubaloff & Associates. Dorothy stared down at the table, I looked at Noel in disbelief, and Noel quickly added, "You have one hour to collect your personal belongings and leave the premises. John, here, will show you out."

Noel gestured toward a uniformed security guard I'd never seen, who had just entered the room. Apparently, Noel hired him for the day in the event there was some sort of physical altercation. I, of course, had no intention of getting into a fight, and the mere suggestion of it was insulting.

I walked numbly to my office, put a few things in the one box they left me, and walked out the door. On the way to my car a man passed me going the other way. He was a locksmith, and he was there to change the locks. Not only had I been thrown out by the partner with whom I'd founded the company and spent many years together, he was making sure I couldn't get back in.

When Dorothy Parker said, "ugly goes clean to the bone," I don't think she envisioned it taking an axe and chopping me to pieces.

Devastated but determined, I immediately called Don Buchwald back in New York to tell him what happened, just as I had kept him informed of any conversations I had with Noel. I said as soon I wrapped things up in Los Angeles, I would be back in New York, and as we'd agreed over dinner and a handshake at the Friars Club, he and I would go into business together. He said, "Fine," and hung up. We were on our way.

Or so I thought.

A couple of months after Noel and Dorothy had performed their palace coup, I indeed went back to New York, as I said I would, to sit down with Don and plan our future together. When we finally met, to my utter astonishment, Don somehow couldn't recall that we had shaken hands on this subject at the Friars Club. At least that's what he told me. But the reality of it was evident.

In the time leading up to my leaving New York, I took Don to lunch and dinner with the important clientele I'd been representing over the years. I did so to transfer their allegiance and loyalty to him, explaining that I was moving to Los Angeles for a year or two, and in my absence, they should look to Don as the person running the New York office.

However, while I was in California, Don had grown close to my clients, as any good agent would do. So close that when Noel fired me, Don came to the realization that, "Well, gee, Harry isn't in the company anymore. I don't need to go into business with him. I'll go into business on my own." To that end, he took my clients, left Abrams-Rubaloff & Associates, and opened an agency called "Don Buchwald & Associates." After all we'd been through and talked about, he'd reneged on our deal. I was furious, but there was nothing I could do.

Except keep moving forward.

Since I still owned 50 percent of Abrams-Rubaloff & Associates, and I no longer had a paycheck, I had to figure out how to get access to my money. I got together with my accountant and hired an attorney to figure out what I could do. Besides getting my equity, could I even form a new company?

I went to SAG to secure a franchise. They said that they certainly would give me one so I could start a new company, but I couldn't use my name because it was already attached to another talent agency.

I said, "I know. That's me. I'm the Abrams in Abrams-Rubaloff & Associates."

They said, "It doesn't matter. You can't use Abrams."

"Why?" I asked. "It's my name!"

"Can't do it," they said. "Already in use as a talent agency."

At that point, I was so angry I didn't even own my own name. Exasperated, I suggested HA Artists Agency, which they accepted. With that, I had a new name. Now I needed artists to represent.

I began to contact some of the clients and employees with whom I'd been working over the years. When Noel heard about this, he became enraged and filed a lawsuit against me to prevent me from approaching anyone associated with Abrams-Rubaloff & Associates.

Chopping me to pieces wasn't enough. He wanted to fry me.

I asked my attorneys what recourse I had. They said I would have to try out a new statute that had come into being and sue Noel to get my 50 percent equity ownership in the company. The statute said that if you have two 50 percent owners of a company and they don't get along, and one of the 50 percent equity owners wants to leave the company, he can offer to sell his equity to the other partner. If the other partner refuses to buy it, the statute says you can force them to liquidate the assets of the company and divide them between the two shareholders.

This then begs the question, what was the value of Abrams-Rubaloff & Associates' assets? The answer was not as easily arrived at as you might think. The court said three appraisers must decide the value. One appraiser was appointed by one side and one appraiser was appointed by the other side, and then those two appraisers got together and selected a third and independent appraiser who had no relationship with either side.

Sound complicated? Imagine being one of those appraisers. They had to talk to talent. They had to talk with past and present employees. They had to talk with competitive talent agencies. They had to speak with accountants. They had to speak with business affairs, and with people from the studios and advertising agencies. They had to look at every conceivable asset.

The assets were a people business with a couple of exceptions. Many years earlier, when I was with Abrams-Rubaloff & Associates, I bought a piece of property in Lake Tahoe with a voice client of ours named Lee Zimmer. Then, after Noel came up to Lake Tahoe a few times and decided he also liked the area, we decided to buy another house from the same builder as an investment. Real estate in Lake Tahoe was booming, and these properties had great value.

After some time, Lee Zimmer wanted to sell his interest in the house we'd bought together. I didn't want to personally buy it, but I thought it would be a good investment for Abrams-Rubaloff & Associates. So we bought it from Lee, which meant we now owned two pieces of property in Lake Tahoe.

We also had a third piece of real estate, which Abrams-Rubaloff & Associates acquired from a director client we represented. We had put him to work directing game shows. He had gotten behind in his bills and hadn't paid his agency commission to us for about a year and a half, which we allowed because he had some financial issues. Finally, we got to the point where we said, "We can't continue to do this. You owe us a lot of money, several thousand dollars."

Since he had a cash flow problem, he offered to give us his small beach house in Malibu. He said, "If you'll assume the mortgage on this home, I'll give it to you in exchange for all of the money that I owe you in commissions." We took that deal, and it was another good financial decision.

In addition to the three pieces of real estate, over the years I had bought some valuable pieces of antique furniture and artworks that were also part of our assets. So when we talk about the assets of the company, there was tangible value involved.

The appraisal took about a year and a half. This was a long, long process for them, and it was on top of the arbitration roadblock Noel had thrown in my way. This was the arbitration case that stipulated I was to have no contact with anyone associated with my former agency including my employees and clients.

Meanwhile, I didn't have an income, I was racking up enormous legal fees, and I was trying to create another business so I could sustain myself and my family. Back in New York, Don Buchwald and my former associates in that office were still working for Abrams-Rubaloff & Associates and I couldn't do anything about it. It was an excruciating time. My anxiety was through the roof, and I was losing hair and weight at a rapid pace.

Finally, after a year and a half, the three appraisers finally reported their findings to the Superior Court judge who had jurisdiction over the case. The judge took a mean average of the three appraisers' values and ordered Noel to pay it. Case closed, right?

Far from it. If either Noel or I didn't like the valuation we could appeal the decision. I had tried to settle on numerous occasions along the way, and when the judge issued his verdict, I accepted it. Noel did not. He dug in even harder and appealed. This meant we would have to go through another year and a half with the Circuit Court of Appeals in the State of California.

After another year and a half, the appellate court confirmed the lower court's decision and ordered Noel to pay up. They also stated that if he didn't pay the value owed to me, they would attach seven percent interest to the amount from that day forward. Quite an incentive for Noel to back down and for the case to be closed, right?

Again, Noel dug in and fought. At the time, interest rates were at an all-time high for savings. Since Abrams-Rubaloff & Associates was getting 12 percent on the money in their savings account, and Noel was only being charged seven percent interest on the money he owed me, it was an easy business decision for him to keep hacking away at me. He appealed to an even higher authority – the Supreme Court of the State of California. This process promised to take another year.

I was at my wit's end. I was alone in New York with a phone, a legal pad, and a nondescript office. But I kept moving forward. I was convinced that the old saying, "The wheels of justice turn slowly, but grind exceedingly fine" would come true on my behalf. I knew I was in the right, but when it would be accepted as true was another matter. And although justice was taking its own sweet time arriving, it was going to come, and Noel would receive his full punishment.

Justice came at long last when the Supreme Court of the State of California, after reviewing all the documents, said the appeal was without merit, they wouldn't even hear the case, and they were confirming the lower court's decision. Finally, it really was case closed. Again, the value was the same as it had been when the first judge took a mean average of the three appraisers' value. The court ordered Noel to pay that value to me within 30 days or sell the company, liquidate the assets, and divide the proceeds between the two of us.

The case, though not the ugliness, was finally over.

Since this was the first case to test the new statute, two UCLA Law School professors used the Abrams versus Abrams-Rubaloff & Associates lawsuit to teach Dissolution of Partnerships and/or

Corporations. They also published a textbook that is still used to teach the statute, so I guess you could say mine was a textbook case of Hollywood ugly. And the fallout from the case continued as more breakups – personal and professional – took place.

In the early 70's, a few months after Roz and I divorced, I ran into a lady friend named Lizbeth Schiff while I was on my way to a therapy appointment in Los Angeles. This was during the time that Noel and I were still together and were at each other's throats over the direction we thought the company should take. It was a trying time, and I was seeing a therapist once a week, as was Lizbeth, whom I had known while I was married to Roz.

Lizbeth and I started spending a lot of time together, and we developed a nice personal relationship. Since she was originally from New York City, and she loved the theatre as much as I did, she came with me to New York to help me find office space – and she stayed.

She said she had never met an agent, and she was impressed by the way I enticed clients and signed them. Although she had an MA in Psychology, and she was a practicing psychologist, she asked me if I could train her to be an agent and work with me. I did, and soon she was working in the office, interviewing potential agents, going to dinner and the theatre with me two or three times a week, and seeing clients and prospects. We worked together like this for two or three years, got closer and closer, and finally, fell in love and got married.

Lizbeth and I were together for ten years, seven of which were as a married couple. We also had a son, Zach.

In my case, when I wanted to move back to New York after the breakup of Abrams-Rubaloff & Associates, Lizbeth and Zach came with me. Lizbeth had been a social worker in Los Angeles, and she became a probation officer for the City of New York. But with me constantly flying back and forth between New York and Los Angeles, making frequent trips to London to scout talent, and fighting with Noel in the courts our marriage didn't survive – another casualty of Hollywood and possibly, of being an entrepreneur.

After our divorce, Lizbeth developed a relationship with another man, got married to him, and took our son with her to London. Luckily, this time it wasn't to a teepee or commune. However, he was part owner of the Boston Celtics which, as a lifelong Lakers fan, was particularly irritating.

As for Zach, he developed a successful career as a film executive then pivoted to working as the COO of Exploding Kittens, a game and entertainment company. I think it's interesting how, after coming from a broken marriage, with parents on separate continents, Zach chose to work and build a company whose mission is to inspire people to connect, laugh and play fun games, together with

Zach

family and friends, in the physical world. As Zach has shared with me, it's possible that he is subconsciously creating the sense of family togetherness for others that he did not have for himself as a child. After helping to navigate the sale of Exploding Kittens, Zach is now working on achieving his personal dream of opening "the best damn restaurant" in Los Angeles. Remember when I said that working for one company your entire career is a thing of the past, Zach is a good example of that evolution.

Back in my talent agency business, after Noel threw me out of Abrams-Rubaloff & Associates, things there began to deteriorate rapidly. One high-profile case was Richard Lawrence, one of our most successful agents. He had been with Les Crane Productions – I'd put Les on the air at KLAC Radio and he'd become a popular late-night broadcaster for the ABC Television Network – and when the show on which Richard worked was cancelled, I hired him and trained him to be an agent. Richard was closely aligned with me, and he was quite upset and disappointed at the way Noel treated me. He decided to leave the company, stop being an agent altogether, and form a personal management company. He took a bunch of Abrams-Rubaloff & Associates clients with him.

In addition to Richard leaving there was a good amount of dissension at Abrams-Rubaloff & Associates. Of those employees who hadn't left outright, many remained who were actively looking for new opportunities. Clients left. Advertising customers and casting directors stopped doing business with the company. Clearly, Noel's reputation was tarnished because of the ordeal.

When I finally received the money Noel owed me – my half of Abrams-Rubaloff & Associates – I was able to move out of the one-person office I'd opened for H.A. Artists and into a new location at 575 Lexington Avenue.

We were a small and scrappy shop, now known as Abrams Artists Agency, with maybe eight to twelve employees. This included a young Neal Altman, our first employee, who remained with the agency for forty years as a senior executive. In those days, I couldn't pay much, but I could do other things to try to let our people know how much I valued their contributions. For instance, I always asked for their opinions on things, and listened, not just for show, but because I really needed them. I took people with me to the theatre, to lunch and dinner, and on client calls. I celebrated their victories. And when somebody lost a client, I didn't focus on the lost revenue. Instead, I tried to pick them up, encourage them, and help them figure out how they could bring in new revenue. It was like a family, and we had fun together.

Let me say one thing about Neal Altman. When I left Abrams-Rubaloff, I hired Neal when I opened my New York office. From his humble beginnings as a young man newly graduated from Brooklyn College with no experience in entertainment, Neal developed into a strong agent in the commercial voiceover department and had a significant contribution in developing Abrams Artists Agency into a premier competitor in this arena, earning us, and our clients, millions of dollars over his long career. He also became part of management, a trusted and loyal advisor. His loyalty afforded me the opportunity to open our LA office and gave me the freedom to spend significant amounts of time building and developing our LA operation. Neal is an example of many young people who began their careers with me, developed into terrific agents and helped me build Abrams Artists Agency. I cannot name them all but I will forever be grateful. Neal was one of three employees who eventually purchased the company with Adam Bold; Brian Cho and Robert Attermann.

In terms of fun, there is one thing that I remember quite fondly. At Christmas, just as the industry was shutting down for the holidays, I would take the staff out to a lunch at a nearby restaurant for a few hours. I would be sure to keep filling everyone's wine glasses. Then they would go back to the office, completely drunk. I would take over reception and answer the phone using one-liners like this: "William Morris Agency" or "Gluck's Plumbing." The staff loved it. No one was working at that point anyway. But they were cracking up and enjoyed watching and listening to me answer the phone with the one-liners. I may have even loved it more than them!

The business flourished, and lo and behold, the Abrams-Rubaloff & Associates office in New York became a mere skeleton of what it once was. Eventually, Noel closed the office.

With Abrams-Rubaloff & Associates no longer in New York, I went to SAG and asked for the rights to change the name of my company to Abrams Artists Agency. I was able to secure that, and I left H.A. Artists behind without a second glance.

I had my name back.

When I think back to the lessons I learned during this period, there were many.

I learned how corrosive anger and resentment can be, and how forgiveness is a crucial personal and business skill. I'm no Mahatma Gandhi, but I believe he was right when he said, "The weak can never forgive. Forgiveness is the attribute of the strong."

From a personal standpoint, if you can't admit your mistakes and forgive others theirs, you are setting yourself up for all kinds of health problems. Unless you can own up to causing harm, and you can let go of wrongs done to you, research has shown you are at risk for a suppressed immune system, depression and anxiety, and a shorter lifespan.

I'm fortunate to have learned this the hard way. Because although I suffered through health problems with my failed marriages and my broken partnership with Noel, I learned my lesson early enough to prevent having a shortened life. Noel, on the other hand, was not as lucky. He died not long after our split, in 1982, at the age of 53. Even though our relationship ended badly, and I had forgiven him his transgressions, I was heartened by the fact that when I went to his funeral, his family embraced me as one of their own.

From a business standpoint, unforgiving and revenge-seeking leaders will spread their emotional toxins throughout their company – at high cost to their employees and to the organization's bottom line. That's because people who are afraid of making mistakes and getting punished for them will become paralyzed and avoid taking calculated risks. And a company filled with people who think and behave like that will not grow; it will wither on the vine.

On the flip side of forgiveness, I learned trust is a two-way street. If you want to be trusted, you must be trustworthy. If people want you to trust them, they must earn your trust. Perhaps you've heard the adage: "it takes a lifetime to build trust and seconds to lose it." I don't exactly agree with that. Trust is eroded in instances large and small, and it's rebuilt in the same way. The passage of time doesn't necessarily have anything to do with it. Doing what you say you'll do does. Giving your word and then going back on it does.

If you're an agent, your reputation for trustworthiness is one of your greatest assets – and liabilities. For instance, in my zeal to build my business and get the best deal for the talent I was representing there were times I tried to change the terms of an agreement at the last minute. This may have been more beneficial to us in the short-term, but it sometimes irritated my advertising clients to the point that they lost trust in me, and I had to work that much harder to regain that trust. Similarly, when Don Buchwald conveniently "forgot" the handshake agreement we made over dinner at the Friars Club, opened his own agency, and took Abrams-Rubaloff & Associates clients and employees with him, he certainly lost my trust. I don't know if he lost the trust of others, because only he and I knew about our agreement.

On the talent side of the business, it is critical to be able to trust the people with whom they're working. This is particularly true for actors and actresses who are vulnerable in ways most of us can't imagine. In service to their craft, they expose their emotions and psyches and bodies while others – most of all, critics – judge them. Although they may seem fragile, and they are, they are also incredibly strong and courageous. After all, who among us could withstand the kind of scrutiny they endure whenever they do their jobs? They deserve all the trust in the world. If their contract says one thing and a director or producer asks them to do another, that's wrong. In return, if their contract calls for them to do something, say, show up to the set sober and on time, and they don't, that's wrong. The same is true with all types of talent, as well as the people with whom they're working. Again, trust is a two-way street, and if you go in the wrong direction, a head-on collision is sure to result.

And what about an entrepreneur or a CEO of a business that's not in the entertainment industry? Is trust important? You bet it is. Otherwise, banks won't lend to them, vendors won't do work for them, partners won't partner with them, communities won't welcome them, the media won't report positively about them, investors won't invest with them, employees won't work for them, and customers won't buy from them. If trust is breached with any of those stakeholders, it is simply bad for business. And yet, we know trust is broken every day. Why? Sometimes it's just a mistake. But in my experience, trust is broken due to one of many factors including greed, vanity, ambition, dishonesty, bad judgement, selfishness, poor decision-making, shortsightedness, expediency, repeated lack of accountability, poor values, and an overall lack of ethics.

Sometimes it's all of the above.

Which brings me back to the entertainment industry and something the playwright, screenwriter and director, another of our former clients, David Mamet, has said, "Life in the movie business is like the beginning of a new love affair: it's full of surprises, and you're constantly getting fucked."

Take it from someone who has regrettably experienced more than one case of copulation. Other than to be sure that you have kick-ass, competent lawyers and trusted advisors on your side, I went with the wisdom from my co-star Hedy Lamarr....

"If you do good, people will accuse you of selfish, ulterior motives. Do good anyway. The biggest people with the biggest ideas can be shut down by the smallest people with the smallest minds. Think big anyway. What you spend years building may be destroyed overnight. Build anyway. Give the world the best you have and you will be kicked in the teeth. Give the world the best you've got anyway."

Regardless of your role or industry, you should do all you can to act ethically and be trustworthy. It's not only the right thing to do; it's good for business. Most important of all, it's good for your soul.

Chapter 12: What's In A Name?

Today, all day I had the feeling
A miracle would happen
I know now I was right.

—Leonard Bernstein and Stephen Sondheim
From *West Side Story*

With the Abrams-Rubaloff & Associates mess behind me, and my second divorce nearly complete, I settled in at the Minskoff Theatre for the 1980 Broadway revival of *West Side Story*, which premiered in 1957. Featuring a book by Arthur Laurents, choreography by Jerome Robbins and Peter Gennaro, and a score by Leonard Bernstein, *West Side Story* transposes Shakespeare's *Romeo and Juliet* to the gang-ridden streets of 1950s Manhattan.

Most importantly for me, *West Side Story* also heralded the Broadway debut of a 27-year-old wunderkind lyricist named Stephen Sondheim, who would go on to change the face of musical theatre with his poetic, playful and powerful lyrics about love, loyalty, hope, revenge, forgiveness, society and class, youth, race and overcoming adversity. He certainly changed my life; he is my all-time favorite theatre artist and I've seen every one of his shows.

My journey as a lifelong Sondheim fan began on that evening in the theatre, when I knew, to quote the great man himself, I'd "find a new way of living."

That new way arrived a few months later in the person of a beautiful and wise young woman named Gay Small, who Walter Kerr could have been writing about in his review of *West Side Story* for *The New York Times*: "Exciting, colorful, edgy with energy."

Gay was working as a commercial producer for an advertising agency, McCaffrey and McCall, which was in the same building as my talent agency: 575 Lexington Avenue, between 51st and 52nd street.

As Gay tells it, one day in front of the building, she bumped into an old friend she had grown up with, Neal Altman, who told her he had just started working as an assistant at Abrams Artists Agency and was excited about his future there. She and Neal were about the same age and their parents knew each other from the housing projects where they both lived in Sheepshead Bay, Brooklyn. When the Mitchell Llama apartments were built for low-to-middle-income housing, many of the Jewish families moved there from the projects, including Neal's family and Gay's. Neal lived in building 1 and Gay lived in building 4, right across the parking lot from each other. They were a very tight knit community.

As I was leaving the building that day, Neal called me over and introduced me to Gay. Since she was producing and buying our talent – through her agency's casting director – for on-camera and radio commercials and voice overs, she knew who I was and was aware of my reputation as a tough and successful negotiator. Our meeting was professional and friendly; nothing more, nothing less.

After that day, I would sometimes bump into Gay on the subway; we both used the Lexington Ave line to get to work. Also, when she was producing, Neal would call her to ask if he and I could come to McCaffrey and McCall to use their production facilities. Our office was small, and since we didn't have equipment to view our client's work, Gay would thread a 16mm film to her projector – later, 3/4-inch video cassettes – for us to screen.

This went on for some time, until one day, I called to invite her to lunch. Normally, I didn't call producers directly and called the casting directors instead. So, she was a bit confused. But she must have assumed I wanted to sell her our talent, because she accepted my invitation to have lunch at a Japanese restaurant on 57th Street called Robata. After about a half hour of small talk, I mentioned that I was separated from Lizbeth and was in the process of getting a divorce. One thing led to another, and we began dating.

We didn't get married for about four years. After two divorces and both wives cheating on me, I was not itching to get married again.

In fact, one time early on in our relationship, as Gay and I were vacationing in St. Barth's, alone – she hadn't even met my boys yet – she asked me out of curiosity if I thought I'd ever marry again. There was really no pressure to the question because I suspected she wasn't sure she wanted to marry a man 20 years older than her who had four children and two failed marriages. And I did not want to get burned again.

I said, "I never say never. But no, never."

In 1985, she became Gay Abrams, and we've been married ever since.

To paraphrase Stephen Sondheim, there was indeed a place for us. So, when I say my life changed after seeing *West Side Story*, it is true in more ways than one.

Back in New York, the Abrams Artists Agency grew like mad. In the 20 years I'd been a talent agent, revenue from television advertising – my specialty – had gone from just over $1 billion to $7.5 billion. By 1977, that amounted to 20 percent of all advertising in the United States – and it was growing exponentially. Every three years the unions renegotiated the commercial contracts with the advertising agencies, and each time the money got bigger and bigger.

We got our fair share of that revenue, and the talent we represented did very well. But while commercials were always a

Gay
credit: Maya Myers

big part of the business, the reality business also grew. So did alternative programming, game shows, reality shows, and docu-soaps. This rapid growth enabled me to do other things, like work in motion pictures, television, and theater. As I said earlier, representing soap opera clients was a natural extension for our business. That's because the programs were closely allied with Procter & Gamble, which was not only a major producer of soap operas but a huge source of television commercial production, and often, they'd hire the same kind of talent.

Within two years of starting Abrams Artists Agency, we were representing about 30 of the biggest soap opera stars in New York and we were the number one agency in that field. With that success, on top of all the other areas in which we were growing, we were a hot ticket. And we hadn't even opened a Los Angeles office.

But it was something else that told me I'd finally made it. That I'd hit the big time. That I was a bona fide, card-carrying "master of the universe."

I received an envelope in the mail one day at my home address. I turned the envelope over and I immediately recognized the stationery because I handled thousands of pieces just like it while I was working at MCA. In gold-embossed lettering on the back of the envelope it said, "Jules Stein, Beverly Hills, California." There was no street address because everyone who worked in the Beverly Hills post office knew where Jules Stein lived and worked.

I stared at the envelope for a long time, finally thinking, "Wow. I only met this gentleman once or twice during the time that I worked at MCA. And one of the times was when I drove up his driveway like an idiot with the gull wing doors to his Mercedes wide open. Why would he be writing me a letter? Has he heard about my success in New York and is writing to congratulate me?"

Now, anyone who knows me at all is aware I have a reputation for being. . .frugal. Okay, cheap. So, when I read the first lines of the letter I nearly fainted.

"Dear Harry, thank you for your $5 million contribution to the Jules Stein Eye Institute. You've chosen a worthy cause. We've always known of and appreciate your philanthropic interest," et cetera, et cetera. He signed off with, "Cordially, Jules."

My first thought was, "What have I done!?"

Then I saw the postscript. "P.S. The next time you're in Beverly Hills, please call Doris and me. We'd love to have you and your wife over for dinner."

I again picked up the envelope and looked at the address.

It was addressed to Harry Abrams all right. But it was supposed to go to a different address where another Harry Abrams lived. And this man, Harry N. Abrams – I'm Harry A. Abrams – was a famous and successful publisher of world-renowned art books. I knew this because, as an art collector myself, I had one on my coffee table.

I obviously received the letter from Jules Stein by mistake. My bubble was burst that he wasn't writing to me, but I was thankful I had not somehow given him $5 million.

The next day I returned the letter to Mr. Stein, and wrote him a brief note. I didn't have the balls to call him "Dear Jules." Instead, I wrote, "Dear Mr. Stein, I worked for your company for about six years and although I had the good fortune to meet you once or twice, I believe the attached letter was intended for the other Harry Abrams. His correct mailing address is on West 57th Street here in New York. I hope someday to be in the position where I would be able to afford a $5 million contribution to the Jules Stein Eye Institute. I really think it's a terrific organization. Cordially, Harry Abrams."

After I signed it, I added a postscript. "However, the next time my wife and I are in Beverly Hills, we'd love to take you and Doris up on your gracious invitation to come over for dinner."

I sent it along. About a year later I ran into his secretary in New York. She said he got quite a chuckle out of my letter.

Despite my humbling experience with Mr. Stein's letter, and of seeing my bank account briefly pass before my eyes, Abrams Artists Agency was firing on all cylinders in New York.

That success, coupled with the equity and interest I'd received from the case with Rubaloff, meant it was time to execute phase two of my plan: expand to Los Angeles.

Just as I'd done when I was fighting with Noel, I made trips to Los Angeles to sell our agency clientele from New York in motion pictures, television, and theater. We would develop the talent in New York, and then place them with an independent agent in Los Angeles. This kind of arrangement was new in the agency business, and it became quite successful. In return for them selling the clientele in Los Angeles, I'd split the agency commission with them.

Over time, I developed corresponding relationships with four or five different talent agencies. One of them was the Gersh Agency, which had two young guys working for them, Howard Goldberg and Scott Harris, both of whom were doing a great job with our clients. As our friendship grew, I saw an opportunity to leverage our relationship to open a new office in Los Angeles, with them running it. Since our New York office was doing so well and I didn't want to move back to Los Angeles, I approached Howard and Scott, and I asked them to come work for me.

Howard and Scott agreed to join me, and once they were on board, we opened an office at 9200 Sunset Boulevard in West Hollywood. The building is one of the top entertainment office properties in Los Angeles and has housed many companies from the industry, including Ford Models, Atlas Entertainment, and Sotheby's auction house. I was proud that location was home to our new company, which we called Abrams, Harris & Goldberg. It was a separate company from Abrams Artists Agency, and I put their names on the door along with mine. Although they weren't partners, I thought it was important that talent see they were running the shop out there since I was staying in New York.

Because Howard and Scott had never run their own business, I flew into Los Angeles regularly to work with them. For the first several months I'd spend a week in Los Angeles and a week in New York. As I grew more comfortable with them and felt they could run things by themselves, I began to come less. I'd stay in New York for two weeks, and then spend one week in Los Angeles. Then, three weeks in New York and one in Los Angeles. Eventually, I only came once every five or six weeks.

By design, we weren't in the commercial or broadcast journalism business in Los Angeles, as we were in New York. Instead, we focused on representing actors and actresses for their work in motion pictures, television, and theater in Los Angeles. We trained younger people to come into the company, including Connie Tavel and Steve Lovett, both of whom became successful personal managers.

Just as we had grown in New York, we quickly grew in Los Angeles. In the entertainment industry, we say a film or a musical or a play has "legs" when it runs longer and is financially more successful than anticipated. While I always thought we'd be a hit in Los Angeles, Abrams, Harris & Goldberg had beautiful legs.

To feed the need for talent in Los Angeles, I began to more actively scout actors and actresses in London. In the same way that I formed corresponding agency relationships in Los Angeles when I was in New York, I did so in London. It was through a contact at one of those agencies that I met an Irish actor who was living and working in London on stage, in television, and in small-budget films. He had recently finished one of those films, *Excalibur*, with Helen Mirren, when I was introduced to him. His name was Liam Neeson.

Liam Neeson

He was in his early to mid-30s when we met, and I took an immediate liking to him. Tall, talented, and ruggedly handsome, he exuded a quiet and humble confidence. In talking with him, I got the sense he truly appreciated his craft, worked hard at it, and had a varied life experience upon which he could draw. He'd been an accomplished amateur boxer in Ballymena, Northern Ireland, where he grew up. He was smart – he'd studied physics at university before leaving at 19 to work as a forklift driver for a Guinness brewery. He'd been a member of the Lyric Players Theatre, in Belfast, and the Abbey Theatre, in Dublin, and he'd been in the world premiere of Brian Friel's *Translations*. Liam also had, and continues to have, a healthy perspective about the entertainment industry. I was not surprised when, long after he'd become a big-time movie star, he said, "For every successful actor or actress, there are countless numbers who don't make it. The name of the game is rejection. You go to an audition, and you're told you're too tall or you're too Irish or your nose is not quite right. You're rejected for your education, you're rejected for this or that and it's really tough." Despite his huge success as an actor, he also doesn't get too full of himself, saying, "Some mornings you wake up and think, 'Gee, I look handsome today.' Other days I think, 'What am I doing in the movies? I wanna go back to Ireland and drive a forklift.'"

Liam Neeson was just the kind of talent I wanted to represent, and I thought he had a tremendous amount of promise. I figured if I could bring him to Los Angeles, help him get a two-year work visa with the United States Immigration and Naturalization Service, and put him in the capable hands of Howard Goldberg and Scott Harris, he could develop a foothold in Hollywood.

He did just that, and the rest is history.

I can't begin to say how many actors and actresses with whom I had similar experiences. Like Connie Britton, who I found at the Sundance Film Festival, Katie Holmes, who was a teen model in Toledo before I got her a part on *Dawson's Creek*, and Dove Cameron, who grew up in Seattle before moving to Los Angeles and working on *Liv and Maddie* for Disney. I share these stories not to name-drop Liam, Connie, Katie and Dove, but to illustrate what went into finding and nurturing talent, providing them with opportunities, and helping them build their careers. Of course, I didn't do this alone...Joe Rice also worked with Connie. Wendi Green met Katie and with Katie's mother, flew to LA to meet with me to discuss the pilot for *Dawson's Creek*. Pam Fisher, another agent, worked with Dove. We worked together as a team at the agency on behalf of our clients.

The reverse is also true. Actors and actresses, writers, directors – everyone on the talent side of the business – go through a virtual hell to find their way in the business. They are like entrepreneurs raising money to start a business except they are the product. Imagine how hard that is. It takes every ounce of ingenuity and persistence and training and sacrifice and networking and other positive attributes to keep selling yourself when rejection is, as Liam Neeson said, the name of the game. But it can be done.

Scouting talent was a common and constant thing for me to do. We would find or develop the talent in New York or in London and bring them to Los Angeles. And so, I continued to go back and forth between Los Angeles and New York throughout this period with Abrams, Harris & Goldberg. And of course, having their names on the door gave them identity. It gave them position. They looked as if they were owners or partners in the company. It made them out to be very strong businesspeople and recognized in the community with the caliber and the quality of the talent. They did an excellent job. And Abrams Artists Agency continued to flourish in New York. As a result, I had to go to Los Angeles less and less.

What happened, however, was that as they got more confidence in themselves, they came to the point where they felt they didn't need me as much anymore. And even though they participated in the revenue of the Los Angeles office, and they were making a lot of money, they wanted to have more of a sense of ownership. I found out later that they also wanted equity.

About four years after we set up Abrams, Harris & Goldberg, they decided to leave the company and form their own business. They never asked me about it or gave me any indication of their plans. It was a traumatic and difficult time for me because I wanted to maintain the office in Los Angeles and keep building it. But when they left, they took whatever clientele and employees would go with them, and they left me hanging. This story was all too familiar, and it hurt me terribly.

The tough thing was I had been planning to talk about giving them equity in the company. But I hadn't done it yet. I misjudged the situation and thought they were satisfied with the way things were. Clearly, they weren't.

We went our separate ways. And just as I had to go to arbitration with Noel Rubaloff, I had to go to arbitration with Howard and Scott. That's because the deals they were making were still part of Abrams, Harris & Goldberg, but since they had no equity in the company, they were redirecting the agency commissions to their new entity, which they called Harris & Goldberg. But that money legally belonged to the agency.

Given what I'd gone through with the legal system I loathed the idea of spending more years and more money in the courts. But this time, I got lucky. The arbitrator heard two days of testimony from me and from them, and after lunch, Howard and Scott's lawyer told my lawyer they wanted to settle. We then negotiated a settlement, which enabled me to continue to participate in whatever money Harris & Goldberg generated on behalf of former Abrams, Harris & Goldberg clients for three more years.

By that time, Scott and Howard were representing not only Liam Neeson, but also Anthony Hopkins, Don Ameche, Lou Diamond Phillips, Estelle Getty, Frank Langella, Jason Priestly, Roddy McDowell and many other name-brand stars. This was the business we'd been building, and we were set to continue growing on that trajectory, but Scott and Howard apparently had different plans. In 1992, they changed Harris & Goldberg to Innovative Artists Talent and Literary Agency, which still exists to this day as Innovative Artists. Sadly, in 1993, Howard Goldberg died from AIDS complications.

Scott Harris then took over as president and continued the company's growth by branching into the areas of voiceover, commercials, beauty, comedy and hosting, and speakers; staying true to their vision of highly experienced agents providing service in an intimate setting.

Since then, Innovative Artists has earned a reputation for service, by promoting their clients before themselves. At the core of Innovative Artists' model, is the strong relationship between agents and clients and a mandate on cross-departmental collaboration.

That should all sound familiar because it's what I taught Howard and Scott. We of course became fierce competitors over the years, and I got great satisfaction every time we competed and beat them, but I wish it hadn't happened the way it did. It was a prime example of how the business was becoming more cutthroat and less enjoyable.

However, one of my strengths is my ability to overcome adversity and keep swimming ahead – like a shark, which only stays alive if it keeps moving. In fact, "the shark" became my nickname. Not because I was a predator with an insatiable appetite, but because I treated staying in perpetual motion as a business strategy. To stay alive and thrive, a shark needs to keep moving. They don't get everything they go after, but it's no matter; they keep going. I did the same. Other agencies were bigger, but I prided myself on being able to outwork, outthink, and out-service any of them. To keep moving, no matter what. Since my agency was often cited as one of the top agencies in the business, this proved to be true.

With my New York office well-staffed and in good shape, I moved back to Los Angeles in 1986 to rebuild our organization. Abrams, Harris & Goldberg was now Abrams Artists Agency, on both coasts, and with a new name came new people. And not just at work.

In 1987, Gay and I had our first daughter, Emily, followed in 1991 by her sister Madeleine whom we mostly call Maddy. Our daughters share the best of both of us regarding Gay's social and political causes and my focus on the business of finding and nurturing talent. Emily, who has volunteered and worked on several political campaigns, is today a Senior Director at Nation Swell, a social impact company. Maddy, the youngest in the family, is following in my footsteps, albeit with a modern spin. As a Senior Talent Manager in the digital media

Maddy

world, Maddy is building brands and creating diverse and lucrative sources of revenue for her clients. I am also thrilled to note that both

Emily

daughters, who were taken to the theater at an early age, continue to be avid theatergoers. I'm very proud to say that all of my children share my appreciation of live theater and for that matter, the arts in general. I am immensely grateful to have had that influence on them.

So, in addition to several much-loved and doted-on dogs that's how my family grew after my return to Los Angeles. Back at the Abrams Artists Agency, in rapid succession I was able to hire Joe Rice, Martin Lesak and Nina Pakula, all of whom were already successful talent agents and knew the industry cold. While all three agents made significant contributions to our company, and all went on to other achievements, I became closest to Joe.

Joe was a real character and had a true zest for life. When he was a child, he moved with his family from Miami, where he was born, to California's San Fernando Valley, where he became a regular dancer on TV's *American Bandstand*. After graduating from UCLA with a bachelor's degree in economics, Joe began his career in the mailroom at the William Morris Agency. He rose quickly, and soon became an agent at the Lew Sherrill Agency, which is where he was when I brought him in. He ran our theatrical department for 28 years, and represented an enormous cadre of actors, including Chris Pratt, Fred Dalton Thompson, Robert Englund, Michael Richards, Paul Adelstein, Stana Katic and Joel Tobeck, before he left to launch his own business—the J.R. Talent Group.

Joe was an ambitious and hard-working guy, and he became a longtime friend. Although his managing style could sometimes differ from mine his work ethic was just as demanding—he believed in his clients and would do anything for them, including bringing them to his house in Laguna Beach for holiday dinners.

With Joe, Martin and Nina on board, Abrams Artists Agency took off. With success came bigger concerns, including how to fairly compensate employees, retain them, and manage the company's finances. For these challenges, I had the "benefit" of learning the value of a dollar early in my life.

Chapter 13: The Value of a Dollar

Oh, Lord, you made many, many poor people
I realize, of course, it's no shame to be poor
But it's no great honor either!
So, what would have been so terrible if I had a small fortune?

—Jerry Bock and Sheldon Harnick
From *Fiddler on the Roof*

At my 75th birthday party, my family and friends took turns, much to my delight, in lovingly roasting me. There were videos, song parodies, speeches, photographs – most poking fun at me in some way – and it was magnificent. They roasted me for my love of the sun, for my marriages, for the way I sleep through performances in the theatre, for my work habits, for my neatness, for my ability to "work a room," for my appreciation for humor and a good story, for the way I drive and take care of my cars, for my enthusiasm for the Lakers, for my foot faults in tennis, for the way I dress, for my positive attitude, for the way I hide chocolate around the house, for my passion for art and music and theatre and films and more.

But the most common roasting target was my frugality. And for that, I was, and still am, an easy mark. However, I must say in my defense, I didn't become cheap just for the hell of it.

I was born in 1935, in Kansas City, Missouri. As any student of history knows, every person alive during The Great Depression was impacted in some way. I'm sure even those who weren't born yet have felt the generational fallout from me, including my family and the people with whom I've worked. I'm not saying growing up during that period is the sole cause of my attitudes about money. But I do believe it's useful to look at my formative years in the light of the times in which they occurred.

My grandparents emigrated to the United States from Eastern Europe in the early 1900s. Like most immigrants of that era, they were looking to escape hardship and realize the promise and prosperity of the new world. They found it in, of all places, Kansas City, Missouri, only to lose it again because of the Great Depression. My father's parents had passed away by the time I was born, and my mother's parents rarely spoke of it, but it had to be withering.

Between 1929, when the stock market crashed, and 1941, when the economy bounced back because of manufacturing war-making materials for WWII, Great Plains states suffered a severe drought. Because of this, the over-farmed and over-grazed land in the nation's "breadbasket" became a giant dust bowl of swirling dirt. There were reports that some of the dirt reached as far as 300 miles into the Atlantic Ocean. Since much of the economy still depended on farming, this had a ripple effect on other non-farming related firms that left massive amounts of people unemployed. At least 25 percent of people were unable to find work. In some communities the number was even higher. Unsure of what to do, families left their homes and land, huddled into makeshift "Hooverville" communities – derisively named after President Herbert Hoover – made of cardboard, scrap metal and wooden crates, and went west.

In his 1939 book *The Grapes of Wrath*, author John Steinbeck aptly described the situation: "And then the dispossessed were drawn west—from Kansas, Oklahoma, Texas, New Mexico; from Nevada and Arkansas, families, tribes, dusted out, tractored out. Car-loads, caravans, homeless and hungry; twenty thousand and fifty thousand and a hundred thousand and two hundred thousand. They streamed over the mountains, hungry and restless—restless as ants, scurrying to find work to do—to lift, to push, to pick, to cut—anything, any burden to bear, for food. "The kids are hungry. We got no place to live. Like ants scurrying for work, for food, and most of all for land."

By the time the Depression was over, 2.5 million people fled the Plains states. By some estimates, as many as 400,000 of them went to California, including my parents, grandparents and two-year-old me, all packed into a Model A Ford. California's economy was stronger than most thanks to electricity generated by the Hoover Dam, the prosperous film industry, and the production of airplanes for France and Great Britain during the beginning of World War II. I have to imagine that California's growing economy, and the opportunity that presented, was what drew my family there.

Once we got to Los Angeles, my mother and father and I, then later my three sisters, and a revolving door of relatives, lived in our tiny, two-bedroom house with one bathroom. I slept on a pull-out couch in the dining room.

On my mother's side of the family, my grandfather found work as a barber at 20th Century Fox. My mother's sister, Fran, worked, at Thrifty Drug Stores. Fran's husband, Harvey, was a buyer for Thrifty Drug Stores. And when my three sisters and I were out of the house, my mother worked as a quality control inspector at Thompson Ramo Wooldridge in south Los Angeles.

On my father's side of the family, my dad worked in various newspaper print shops. His three brothers were professional gamblers. I don't mean they liked to gamble; I mean that's what they did for a living. They played cards, bet on horses, you name it. If it had odds, they bet on it.

I guess this means I had competing influences: on one hand, my family watched every penny because we were broke, and on the other, they took a lot of calculated risks trying to turn those pennies into dollars.

As a result, I had to learn what a dollar could and couldn't buy by paying rent and working every waking hour I wasn't in school. This led to a scarcity mentality that stayed with me all my life – though I can't say I was conscious of it. I've only learned of some of these things in the writing of this book.

For instance, when I would get home from one of the many jobs I held as a kid I'd discover that my sisters had eaten all the food from dinner and didn't leave any for me. Instead of complaining, I went hungry. This followed me when, as an adult, I often hid chocolates around the house so my wife and kids wouldn't get to them before me. Other times I chastised my children when they ordered appetizers in a restaurant and didn't eat them. Or when they didn't finish what was on their plate.

Let's Do Launch

In one embarrassing episode, I took my family and my wife's parents out to dinner at a nice restaurant, and when we were getting ready to leave, I insisted that the waiter scrape every bit of food on every plate into doggie bags so we could take the food home and "get more meals out of it." My wife was mortified.

Then there were our family vacations to the Hamptons, a group of towns, villages, and hamlets on the eastern end of Long Island in New York state. The Hamptons are a beautiful stretch of beaches in a rural setting with old farmhouses, spacious mansions, fantastic restaurants, exclusive boutiques, and tony events like horse shows and auctions. Many of the people with whom I did business – ad agency owners, attorneys, bankers, producers, directors, and famous actors and actresses – all went "out east." As the owner of a well-known and successful talent agency with offices in Los Angeles and New York, it made sense for us to vacation there. Plus, we loved the ocean, the beach, and whatever else the Hamptons had to offer.

This begs the question: how does a guy with a scarcity mentality vacation among the rich and famous? First, I wasn't even aware I had a scarcity mentality. Second, I had a burning desire to be successful, and if that's where the movers and shakers went, well, that's where I was going to go.

How I went about it was at once a running gag, a gamble, and a game. Instead of doing what most people did – book a place for the summer maybe a year in advance – I waited until the very last minute. And when I say the last minute, I don't mean a month prior, or even a week.

One week before our summer was to begin, I would leave my family in Los Angeles and take a red-eye flight to the Hamptons myself – without having secured a place for us. Once there, I'd rent a car and drive around looking for places to stay in which the renters of a particular property had, for some reason, backed out of their arrangement. When renters did that, they left the people who owned the property with a huge problem – the possibility of an empty house and lost revenue during their most lucrative part of the year. When I learned of this dynamic, which happened every year, I swooped in at the last minute and negotiated a much lower price, thus "saving" the homeowner's summer. Once I was successful in securing a place for the summer I called my wife, gave her the address, and told her to get on the next plane. Then I'd go to the store, stock up on groceries and other household essentials, and wait to move in.

This was a high-stakes game that I always won. My family and friends thought I was crazy, and that this was one of the many quirks of my personality that endeared me to them. Perhaps both of those are true. As I've said, I can be complicated.

Though I didn't like it at the time my early lessons in finances stuck with me. Throughout my career I've told agents, actors and other entrepreneurs they'll not only have to do with meager incomes when they're starting out, they'll also have to know their worth and market value.

This all had an impact on how I negotiated, how I compensated people, and how I attracted and retained – and sometimes lost – employees. The dueling influences of saving and spending are how I could scrutinize an employee's expenses while buying expensive artwork and antiques for the office. It's how I could pick up paperclips from the carpet while buying enough tickets to see 10 shows in five days. And in the case of Harris and Goldberg, it's how I could neglect to give them ownership in my business while taking the risks of being a business owner myself. The contradictions in my behavior are numerous.

My long-time accountant was one of my closest friends, Ed Astrin, who I'd known since we were fraternity brothers at UCLA. When my wife would express anxiety over how my business was doing and whether we could make it when we were facing a challenging economic time Ed would tell her, "Gay, it's Harry we're talking about. Trust him. He knows what he's doing. It'll all work out."

I'm not entirely sure I knew what I was doing, and I wish I hadn't had to go through the anxiety and the insecurities and the legal fees and the toll it took on my body and my mind to learn these things. But it certainly taught me a lot. As time went on, I became more generous with salaries, bonuses, and participation in the business. This didn't stop one or two key employees from leaving each year – I couldn't compete with a larger agency that was willing to pay an employee twice what I was paying them – but it did lessen the flow.

I will say it can be hard to figure out where people's thinking is in terms of their future and what they want to do and how much they want to make. A lot of that fell on my shoulders, but also it fell on the shoulders of the department heads to retain our agents.

For my part, I tried to maintain a good relationship with everyone in the office. I knew all their names. I knew their families. I knew what was going on in their lives. I interacted with them during the year. Until the day I retired, at least as far as the Los Angeles office was concerned, I approved of and got to know any new person joining the company. If they were in the agent-in-training program, I stayed on top of the department head to see how they were spending their time, what progress they were making, and whether they should be moved into other areas of representation. I took them with me to the theater, to seminars, symposiums, festivals, and conventions. I had a good, strong relationship with my employees because it was important for them to know they had a connection with me as a person and mentor and leader, not some boss giving orders from on high.

Over the years many former employees have said how much they appreciated my hands-on approach and how the example I set influenced the way they do business. Just the other day, for example, the head of our theatrical department in New York, Paul Reisman, talked about how he looked up to me and appreciated how I taught him and nurtured him and treated him like a member of my family. He recently left the agency, and although I'm not sure what he's going to do I know it will be good.

I think of Paul Weitzman, who started our literary department, and after I departed, left to open his own successful literary agency. He has remarked how I am "one of a kind" and learned a lot from the positive way I treated people.

I think of Amanda Marzolf, a young agent who, under the able leadership of Alec Shankman, helped make our digital department the biggest revenue producer in the agency. She recently talked about how shocked and touched she was when I took her and some other new agents out to dinner and the theatre soon after they started. She couldn't believe that I, the CEO, took the time to get to know her and her colleagues when they were just starting out with the company. Amanda is now a partner at Underscore Talent Management.

Jason Alexander

I cannot begin to describe how gratifying it is to know I have had a positive impact on so many people. It also bothers me that I must have also had a negative impact on some people, though hopefully not very many. In my defense, when it comes to money, old habits die hard. But as I've also learned, old habits can be broken.

I believe everyone should be financially literate regardless of which industry or stage of their career they're in. But those launching a career in the arts, and the people who represent those artists, face additional challenges beyond that of more "traditional" people in the workforce. That's also true for entrepreneurs, who share many commonalities with those in the arts, including fluctuating income, uncertain cash flow, an unhelpful mindset, and the need to continually sell themselves.

Let's start with mindset.

As I've said, it would have been helpful for me to be aware I had a scarcity mentality when I began my career. If I knew that was my mindset going into nearly every interaction I had with people or in how I budgeted and spent money I would have been well on my way to financial wellness a lot sooner in my life. And I would have saved myself and everyone around me a lot of heartache and headache.

In the entertainment industry too many people believe in, even if they're not aware of it, the mythical romance of the starving artist. They think the more commercial something is the less artistic value it has. Or conversely, the more independent something is, the greater the artistic value. I'm speaking mostly of talent, of course. And I can tell you that those who were once starving artists and are now financially more successful sincerely wish they did not have to experience being continually broke early in their careers. There was nothing romantic about it.

Take Jason Alexander, for example, a former client of mine. Jason was a classically trained actor from a great program at Boston University. He longed to come out of college and play a meaty dramatic role like Hamlet. When one of his professors said he should think instead about playing a comedic role like Falstaff, in part, because of his stature, Jason was at first indignant. Then he thought about it, and said, maybe he's right.

However, as an actor trained to play serious roles, as unimaginable as it is to say this about one of the comedic geniuses of our time, Jason Alexander – future Tony winner, Grammy winner, four-time SAG award winner, and seven-time Emmy nominee – did not believe he had the ability to be funny. And for the next few months he began a self-taught course of study in how to be funny. He watched old Marx Brothers and Three Stooges movies, television clips of Jack Benny and

Red Skelton, and comedians in clubs. And to support himself financially, he did television commercials. He said if he did one or two a year it was enough for him to live on as he pursued other work. And if you ask him which type of work has more artistic value he will say, "They're all acting, and all acting has value!"

Another actor I represented, William H. Macy, came to me early in his career, after he'd been a "starving artist" doing theatre with David Mamet in Chicago, and asked for a list of all the commercial casting directors and producers I worked with in New York. He wanted to call on them and get work for himself – before I even agreed to represent him! I smiled at his naivete and asked him, since what he described was exactly how I made a living, why would I want to give up these valuable contacts without getting anything in return? He said, "We'll both do it. I just want the work!" I gave him a list anyway because I admired his willingness to work and his positive attitude. And although he never got any commercials by calling on the names of the people I gave him, I did get him work in commercials and theatre and television. Which all helped him financially.

When I spoke with Bill about his career recently, which includes two Emmy awards, four SAG awards, an Academy Award nomination, and his recent amazing 11-year run in the Showtime hit series, *Shameless*, he said if there had been a place he could go to get less "artistic" work and yet reliably pay his bills he would have said, "Sign me up!" We found him that place in television commercials, of which he did plenty.

These two accomplished artists were actors, agents, and entrepreneurs all rolled into one.

Like agents and entrepreneurs, they wanted to make money and have their work be of high artistic value. That's a good mindset to have.

They somehow knew at an early age, as I learned over time, that it's difficult to thrive if you're financially stressed and insecure. It's hard to bring your best into an audition or a new business pitch if you're desperate to get the job – not because you really want it, but because you NEED the money it would bring.

The most important thing you can do right now is to take a close look at your relationship with money. How do you feel about it, and think about it? Does it scare you or excite you? Do you have a positive

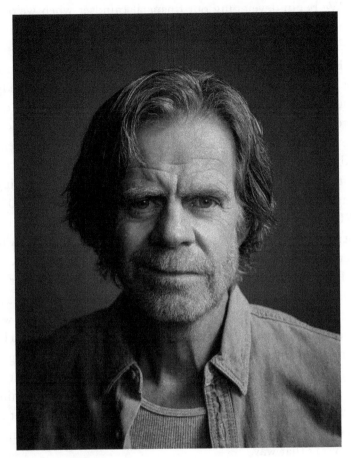

William H. Macy

mindset about money, or a negative one? Our financial wellness is something we have to care for just like we do our bodies and minds and spirits. And it's not "one and done." We can't say we're financially well if we stick to a budget for one day no more than we can say we're physically well because we ate a salad at lunch. Financial wellness is a lifelong pursuit.

We begin developing our financial mindset when we're young. During the early years of our lives, our financial conditioning is greatly influenced by the people around us.

Relative to money and finances, what beliefs did my family have about money? How did those beliefs cause my parents and grandparents and aunts and uncles to act – did they save, did they spend, did they equate financial success with being a good person or did they think money was a corrupting influence? As I've said, my parents and grandparents lived through the Great Depression which created a scarcity mindset rather than a prosperity mindset. Now, having lived through several recessions, the financial crisis of 2008 – 2009, and COVID-19, you may also unwittingly be conditioned to have a negative financial mindset. It's best to examine it now so it's not perpetuated in your life and passed on to the next generation.

Here's another thing: When Mark Twain said, "Never discuss politics or religion in polite company," he could have just as easily added, "or money." While that may be good advice – no one wants to hear someone brag about how much money they have or preach about their religion or spout polarizing politics at a party – following it leads to an unhealthy outcome: we don't talk about it. We keep it hidden away like a dark family secret. With that as our conditioning, it's understandable that we may not have developed a mindset that enables us to deal with finances in a healthy way. But that doesn't mean we have to stay that way.

If you didn't learn the basics of personal finance growing up – how to balance a checkbook, how to properly use credit and credit cards, how to manage cash, how to budget and pay bills – you can learn it now. In fact, you must learn it now, as well as how to invest your money so it works for you over the long run.

One way to get started is write down what you believe about money. Be honest with yourself. Which of these beliefs is self-defeating or limiting? Are any of the beliefs on your list positive and expansive? Do any of them reflect what you'd like your money mindset to be? Now reconcile those lists into one list of positive beliefs that you'd like to embody. Keep your list close to you. When you're having a negative thought about money – you'll begin to realize when you are – pull out the list, look at it, and read it to yourself out loud. Who cares if you don't believe it yet? You've heard the saying, "Fake it 'til you make it?" You do that until you DO believe it. Then, because you're a lifelong learner, you'll continue to keep the list with you at all times.

Jim Carrey did a version of this when he wrote a check to himself for $10 million for "acting services rendered," dated it 10 years into the future, and put it in his wallet. It nearly fell apart with all the wear and tear of him taking it out and looking at it, but his dream for himself came true – many times over. I've never asked him, but I'd be willing to bet he did some self-examination before he even got to the point of writing himself the check.

It's up to each person to learn and develop the tools they need to be financially healthy. I learned by trial and error, but today there are many more resources to rely on. For instance, the Actors Fund has a Financial Wellness Program that engages, educates, and empowers performing arts and entertainment professionals about the role of money in their lives. I recommend everyone participate in the program – and join the Actors Fund or at least contribute to it financially because they do such good work.

The Financial Wellness Program can help you identify your financial goals and get clear about where you're starting from; learn and begin to implement specific strategies for organizing expenses, balancing multiple sources of income and planning for dry spells; understand the elements of your credit report and score, and how to build and maintain healthy credit; develop a savings plan along with skills to begin to engage in the world of investing; gain clarity around debt management and potential repayment and relief options; examine the behaviors and thinking patterns that impact your financial habits and begin to align your actions and intentions.

Now that we've talked about mindset, let's discuss how to set financial goals and get specific about how money flows in our lives. This financial planning and budgeting, and the mindset I spoke of earlier, is kind of like what I went through when I worked with a counselor at UCLA to understand my strengths and plot a course for my future. Except this time, it's regarding money.

Okay, where to start? Now, what I'm about to impart is a basic philosophy about dollars and cents and how to put yourself in a position to move ahead. You're free to use an app or Quicken or any technological element you may find helpful, but I think you'll see the basic underlying concepts remain the same. So, here goes.

First, you need to know how much you're worth. Not in a psychological sense – in that regard, your worth is incalculable. I'm talking about your net worth, which is what you own minus what you owe. For example, you may own a car and a home, but you may also have a car loan and a mortgage. That means your car and home are both assets and liabilities. Other assets may be savings accounts, investment accounts, art, jewelry, antiques and so on. Other liabilities may include credit card debt, school loans, a second mortgage, etc.

Next, you need to figure out an average of how much you make and spend each month. This income minus expenses is your profit and loss statement. While creating this will fill many people with dread, it's a critical step to knowing where you are financially. You may someday have "people" who do this for you, and I hope you reach that point, but even then, it's important that you know what they're doing.

You can start building your profit and loss statement by looking at all your receipts and bank and credit card statements for the past six months. Your receipts may be wadded-up balls of paper. It doesn't matter, at this point. Once you know you'll have to rely on them to tally up your spending, you'll take better care of them. Take what you have and arrange them in categories, personal versus business. And be as detailed as possible. Categorizing something as "food," for example, won't cut it. Delineating food as Starbucks, Pizza, Restaurants, Groceries, Alcohol, etc, is more accurate. "Entertainment" may be Films, Theatre, Concerts, Comedy Clubs and so on. Get the picture?

Then, by adding up each category and dividing by six you'll be able to see how much you spend, on average, each month.

Next, look at the earnings side of your ledger. How much income did you bring in during the last six months? Again, organize that income by categories. For example, if you're an actor, the categories may include bartending, being in a play, doing a voice over, teaching, performing a cabaret show, appearing in a television show or film, and so on. Then you take all that income and divide it by six. That number represents your average monthly income. Calculating this over a year is even better, considering the ebbs and flows of work you may have to deal with. If you're an entrepreneur – again, everybody should think of themselves that way – it's the same dynamic. Your work may be seasonal. Averaging your income over a year gives you a more accurate result.

Now, subtract how much money you spend from how much money you earn and you've got your P&L. If you made $20,000 over the last six months and spent $21,000 your "business" is "running at a loss" or "in the red." If you made $20,000 and spent $19,000 your business is profitable or "in the black."

You may wonder why I'm spending so much time on this. It sounds so fundamental.

Well, you'd be surprised at the "magical thinking" many people have when it comes to money. Having unrealistic attitudes and habits around money is how entrepreneurs may have great ideas but go out of business because their "burn rates" – how much and how fast they spend money versus how much and how fast they bring it in – are so high.

It happens with performers, too. There are countless sad stories of athletes who signed huge professional contracts after college, immediately went on a spending spree because they thought the money spigot would always keep flowing, sustained a career-ending injury, and ended up financially destitute.

Then there are entertainers who didn't try to understand or keep an eye on what their financial advisors and managers were doing with their money, and as a result, lost millions. It makes me sick, when I think of the convicted felon, Bernie Madoff, and the money he swindled from people I know and respect. And there are a lot more just like him, including business and personal managers, who have had to be sued for mismanaging and stealing funds.

If those examples are too extreme, think of the pure anxiety and helplessness of not knowing what's going on with your money. It's terrible.

I believe growing up poor worked in my favor. I'm not trying to spin a bad situation; I mean it. Each month, I saw my mother and father figure out, by looking at how much we spent versus how much we brought in, how we were going to survive. I saw them save to buy things that were important, and bypass things that might have been nice to have but were not necessary. In my paper-selling business and lawn-mowing business I kept detailed records of who owed what, when I needed to collect, what I spent on supplies, how much I owed the newspaper companies, how much I had to pay my employees, and more. All because my father said I needed to work and contribute to the mortgage. Which he didn't say because he was being mean, but because he saw that our family was coming up short financially, and he knew I could close the cashflow gap with a little bit of work. Of course, he also had me work so I could learn the value of a dollar and develop financial literacy.

I also believe I benefitted from working in an industry with fluctuating income. It taught me the importance of planning and taking seasonality into account. For instance, I learned that producers and casting agents would need actors for television pilot season. That was good for the actors I represented and good for my business. On the other hand, if the writers went on strike and no pilots were being produced that could be bad for my actors and for my business.

Outside of the entertainment industry people have ignored financial fluctuations at their peril. People got burned by real estate investments, and the financial derivatives that were created from those investments, when they assumed their money would continue to grow unabated. They didn't consider the broader economic reality and how those investments could come crashing back to earth like they did. If you assume fluctuations will happen as a natural course of doing business, and you anticipate unknown factors will upend your business from time to time, you will plan and act accordingly.

When it comes to finances, everyone in business, regardless of whether they're in the entertainment industry or not, can benefit from those of us who are.

Chapter 14: Diversity and Diversification

So, if you care to find me
Look to the western sky!
As someone told me lately
Everyone deserves the chance to fly!

—Stephen Schwartz
From *Wicked*

Like society at large, for many years agenting was dominated by white males. The same was true for actors, actresses, directors, producers, writers, dancers, and people in business.

When I started at MCA in 1958, there was a grand total of three female agents in the whole agency—one in Los Angeles, and two in New York City. The two in New York were there because of the theatre. The management of MCA thought that since many of the actors, playwrights, composers, and producers were gay it would be best to have women wooing them. It's amazing to me to think how short-sighted, limiting, and bigoted that was for all involved.

To succeed, any business needs to diversify so their employee base mirrors that of their customers. If the agent or talent is good and marketable, why would you not want to work with them? It makes no sense to me. That's why, when I was able to represent talent and hire agents, I vowed to do my part to rectify that situation.

One of the most rewarding signings I made in this regard was the actor, musician, and Down Syndrome advocate, Chris Burke, who played Corky Thatcher on the ABC Television Network series, *Life Goes On*. The pilot referenced Chris who became the face of Down Syndrome.

The show ran for four years before being syndicated around the world for many years thereafter.

When Chris was born, the hospital told his parents that he should be put in an institution. They disagreed, brought him home, and gave him a mainstream life experience, nurturing his talents and interests at every step of his development, including supporting his desire to be an actor and musician. Their stance obviously paid off. As Chris said in an interview, "It's not about performing disabilities. It's about performing abilities."

Following that starring role, after several seasons on TV, Chris appeared in numerous television shows and movies, made personal appearances, and became a spokesperson for Down Syndrome at conventions and festivals throughout the world. I'm truly proud of him and grateful we got a chance to work together.

The story of Chris Burke is just one way to look at the importance of diversity and diversification. To explain it further, I'm going to come at it from a little different angle and give a more holistic perspective on the topic.

One of the things I love about California is its diversity. Everyone knows that without leaving the state, you can ski in the mountains and swim in the ocean on the same day. But that's superficial. And it's not the kind of diversity I'm talking about.

According to World Population Review, an independent organization that measures diversity across six categories – socioeconomic, cultural, economic, household, religious, political – California is the most populous and diverse U.S. state. It ranks first for cultural diversity, having the highest linguistic diversity and the second-highest racial and ethnic diversity; third for socioeconomic diversity; fifth for household diversity; and eighth for political diversity.

In terms of the economy, California is also incredibly diverse, with Hollywood, Silicon Valley, manufacturing, and agriculture all making significant contributions. If California, which makes up 14 percent of the U.S. economy, were its own nation, it would be the fifth largest economy in the world. With a GDP of $2.9 trillion, California would slot between Germany and the United Kingdom in the world's top economies.

In addition, California is a biodiversity hot spot. Because of its unique geography, climate, geologic history and size, California has more diverse species and ecosystems than anywhere in the U.S. This is important because California's biodiversity supports ecosystem services that benefit people and the economy, including carbon sequestration, timber production, crop pollination, soil fertility, tourism, and recreation. And the greater the biodiversity of ecosystems the more stable and resilient they are to pressures and climate change.

These principles extend to people and careers regardless of which industry they're in. In fact, diversification is more important today than ever, because we live in an increasingly uncertain world.

This notion is supported by a resurgence in use of an ancient simile derived from nature — "as rare as a black swan" — which was popularized by Nassim Nicholas Taleb, a finance professor, writer, and former Wall Street trader who wrote about the idea of a black swan event prior to the 2008 financial crisis in his 2007 book titled *The Black Swan: The Impact Of The Highly Improbable.* Taleb's examples of black swan events are the rise of the internet, the personal computer, World War I, the breakup of the Soviet Union, and the September 11, 2001 attacks.

In the book, Taleb argued that because black swan events are impossible to predict due to their extreme rarity, yet have catastrophic consequences, it is important for people to always assume a black swan event is a possibility, whatever it may be, and to try to plan accordingly. In my view, embracing the principle of diversity is one of the best ways to protect yourself and your business when a black swan event does occur.

The novel coronavirus — more commonly referred to as COVID-19 — and its rapidly developing variants is the most obvious recent example of a black swan event. Others include the devastating wildfires, superstorms, earthquakes, and floods caused by climate change; and the insurrection by violent extremists at the U.S. Capitol.

So how can we apply the principles from our natural world to our businesses and careers?

Without question we must employ a diverse workforce. More than the right thing to do, it's an economic imperative. To that end, research from SCORE, a nonprofit organization dedicated to helping small businesses get off the ground, grow and achieve their goals through education and mentorship found that diversity leads to better financial performance, more innovation, faster and better decision-making, and greater attraction and retention of employees. SCORE's research relied on sources such as Boston Consulting Group, Forbes, Harvard Business Review, MIT, McKinsey & Company, Deloitte, Glassdoor and Cloverpop so I know it's high quality. Moreover, I've spent my life and career doing similar work to SCORE's, albeit with talent, talent agents and businesses, so their research resonates with me.

Let's look at some of the impacts of diversity.

In terms of financial performance, gender-diverse companies are more likely to outperform those that aren't by 21 percent, and that number goes to 33 percent for ethnically diverse companies. Companies that aren't diverse are 29 percent more likely to underperform.

Regarding innovation, companies with above-average diversity practices earn 45 percent of their revenue from innovation versus 26 percent from companies with below-average diversity. What's more, companies with more diverse management teams have 19 percent higher revenue because of innovation.

What about decision making? Diverse teams make decisions twice as fast with half the meetings and 60 percent better outcomes. Who can argue with that!?

When it comes to attracting and retaining employees, 67 percent of job seekers say a diverse workforce is an important factor when evaluating job opportunities. Once employees are hired and inside the organization, 57 percent think their company should be more diverse in hiring and 72 percent will leave if they find a more diverse organization.

No less an authority than the World Economic Forum agrees. In 2019, they published a paper titled *The Business Case for Diversity in the Workplace is Now Overwhelming*. I suggest everyone read it.

In addition, without diversity you're also at a disadvantage with your development of products and services, your supply chain and distribution system, and even your acquisitions.

That's right, whether you're selling lawnmowers, your acting clients, or your own talents, if you don't have diversified offerings, you'll put yourself at risk. I'm not talking about engaging in areas that have nothing to do with you. I'm talking about not painting yourself into a corner with one single product or service.

What does that have to do with the entertainment industry? Let's say you're a film or television actor and no one is producing anything because of a writer's strike or a shutdown due to COVID-19. Can you record voice overs at home? Can you teach over Zoom? Can you write for publications? Raise money for something you want to produce? Use your imagination – as an actor that's one of your strengths. How about if you're a talent agent in that situation? What can you do? You can assist the literary department or the digital department, both of which may not be as affected by what's going on. You can work the phones to build and strengthen relationships. You can also teach over Zoom. You are resourceful – as an agent that's one of your strengths. If you're an agency head, you can develop many different lines of business, give your employees experience in different departments, and acquire businesses that fill gaps in your offerings so that when something happens – and it will happen – you have somewhere else to turn.

I began this chapter talking about nature because nature can teach us a lot. After all, businesses – and people – are living organisms. Diversity creates resiliency and healthier ecosystems, no matter the industry.

Let's talk about some of the black swan events I've encountered in my career, starting with labor actions. In early 1960, when I was a young agent at MCA, both SAG and the Writers Guild of America (East and West) went on strike against the Association of Motion Picture Producers. Well, seven of the eight major studios, at least. The eighth was Universal, which came to an agreement before the strike and was later bought by MCA.

It lasted for 146 days, making it the second longest strike ever held by both unions. The dispute centered on broadcast royalties for films that aired on television. Actors demanded a pension and welfare fund, and six percent or seven percent of the gross earnings from pictures made since 1948 and sold to television. Writers wanted a health and welfare fund, five percent of the studio's income from pre-1960 movies that were sold to television, two percent on post-1960 movies, and a raise in their minimum wage.

This was the first industry-wide strike in the 50-year history of movie making. Through two World Wars and the Great Depression, the industry had never ground completely to a halt. It was definitely an unpredictable event.

In December 1978, members of SAG went on strike for the fourth time in its 45-year history, joining AFTRA, with which it later merged, on picket lines in New York and Los Angeles.

In 1980, SAG, AFTRA and the American Federation of Musicians all went on strike and boycotted that year's prime-time Emmy awards.

There have been several other serious work stoppages due to strikes, including the Writers Guild of America strike which lasted 14 weeks, from November 2007 – February 2008. Through them all, I saw successful ways of dealing with strikes, such as how MCA pursued a strategic diversification process long before the strike and were thus able to deal with it more effectively when it did happen. And unsuccessful, such as when Noel Rubaloff dug in his heels and refused to diversify beyond the commercial business, which hurt us badly during the 1978 commercial strike by SAG and AFTRA against the advertising agencies and commercial production companies.

We, Abrams-Rubaloff & Associates, couldn't put any of our clientele to work because we were on the side of labor – and I was happy to be on that side. We lost a lot of money because we supported the unions, but that wasn't the problem. The problem was we failed to diversify.

I said to myself at the time, if I'm able to get through this strike and still survive and still be able to run a business and have a company, even though we have no revenue and no income coming in for several months, I'm going to try to design a business model where I'm not going to suffer like this in the future. I vowed to design an agency with different departments, different areas of the business where the labor union contracts expire at different times.

For example, the commercials contract is a totally different labor-union contract than the one for actors and actresses who work in motion pictures and television. The contract for Actors' Equity Association, which is for performers who work on stage, is a totally different three-year contract than those two other labor-union contracts. The Writers Guild contract is a totally different contract than those three contracts.

The AFTRA contract dealing with newscasters, sportscasters and radio personalities is a different contract than the other four contracts. By different, I mean they expire at different times. They don't all expire concurrently. The soap opera contracts, soap operas fall under AFTRA's union jurisdiction because it covers live taping or videotaping. It's not shot on film. That's a totally different contract than the other contracts.

Diversification was a smart business strategy because it meant that we, as an agency, could survive a strike or work stoppage in one area because we could make up the difference in another area. It meant we weren't going to go out of business. We had diverse revenue streams coming in, agency commissions from other resources, other areas of the business, and we could sustain ourselves and be able to pay the rent, pay the telephone bill, pay the salaries, and so on.

In addition, diversifying helped us protect our clientele because we could find them work in areas that would not compromise their positions in the strike or work stoppage. In other words, we could help them get work without them having to cross a picket line and betray their colleagues. This all made us that much more valuable to them.

In that vein, it's also important to diversify geographically. I've already talked about how I scouted talent in London and developed corresponding relationships with agencies there. I did the same thing with Larry Goldhar, who founded The Characters Talent Agency in Toronto and ran it for 50 years. We first met when I looked him up while I was attending the Toronto Film Festival. Larry's talent agency had always been one of the top three in Canada, and I thought we might be able to do business together. This was confirmed when I discovered we shared the same philosophy of putting our clients first and supporting them and their work. We decided we wouldn't worry about what other agencies did; we'd do our own thing, and we'd excel at it. The relationship worked well for both of us.

Larry's daughter Jennifer Goldhar is now running the business, so I know it's in good hands.

In addition to diversification being necessary for growth of the business, having multiple lines of business was a good employee attraction and retention strategy. We could offer employees and prospects a range of opportunities that would help them see what departments they liked or even if they wanted to remain in the agency business at all.

As I've said, an important way that an agency flourishes is with the expansion into different departments. In our case, we went beyond the commercial department or acting department and developed alternative programming, reality, literary and youth departments.

One important hire to our literary department was Ms. Manal Hammad, a first-generation American of Palestinian descent who we brought on to represent writers and directors from diverse backgrounds. Manal joined us from another agency and made it a priority to look for literary talent that was underrepresented in society. She was instrumental in bringing in a significant roster of diverse clients, including women, and younger, unproven talent who had yet to make their mark. Manal credits my wife, Gay, for giving her the support she needed to take on this difficult task. But Gay will be the first to say that, as outspoken and committed to diversity as Manal was, nothing was going to stop her. Manal left shortly after I sold the agency and joined the Verve talent and literary agency, where she started a theatrical literary department. To give you an idea of how much Manal meant to my agency and to me personally, I've written to the management at Verve to congratulate them on starting their theatre department and to tell them how lucky they are to have Manal running it.

The only acquisition I ever made was a children's talent agency, which became our youth department. Tina DeVries came with the acquisition, and I asked her to stay with us as vice president of Talent Payment. She did, for about 20 years, as one of four vice presidents on our management committee.

Another good example of that was our expansion into the new media and digital arena. This was an area that had never existed in our earlier years because obviously we didn't have computers or the internet then. But I was one of the first talent agents to see where the whole new media and digital arena was going and assigned agents to do nothing but focus and specialize on that area of the business. I asked a young agent named Alec Shankman to take on that department and he was wildly successful at it.

We expanded that department time and again in the specialization of representing "influencers" – talent who had developed hundreds of thousands, even millions, of followers on Instagram, Twitter, Tik Tok and other social media platforms. In turn, these influencers could be marketed to manufacturers of products and services for hundreds of thousands of dollars. We were even able to take some of our talent we represented as actors and actresses and were able to turn them into influential social media influencers. It was a virtuous cycle.

An area of the business we did not move into is personal appearances, concerts, the music business, the recording business, stand-up comedy, and nightclubs. That area of the entertainment industry didn't appeal to me. It's not something with which I wanted to be associated. I couldn't see myself hanging out at nightclubs in Las Vegas or Atlantic City until 2:00 or 3:00 o'clock in the morning with a vocalist or a stand-up comic or whatever. It wasn't my cup of tea. Other agencies have moved into it in a big way and been successful. It's a lucrative end of the talent agency business, but it requires a certain type of an agent to be successful in that area. And my agents and I were never going to be that type of agent.

Another black swan event was the financial crisis of 2008 – 2009. People call it the "Great Recession," but after living through the Great Depression, I hesitate to put the word "great" in front of a recession. Whatever you call it, it had a huge impact on the entire economy, us included.

Broadcast journalists in local television stations were heavily impacted. As one of their agents, I negotiated big contracts for them. But as the economy shrank so did their contracts. That is, if the journalists were fortunate enough to even keep their jobs.

One prominent fellow who retired during the economic crisis was the broadcast journalist Paul Moyer, from KNBC in Los Angeles. He had been a fixture in Los Angeles news for 37 years, and he was probably making $7 million or $8 million a year. However, when his employment contract expired, and they wanted him to take a pay cut of several million dollars per year, he retired.

That's just one example, but it took place all over the market, not only in Los Angeles and New York and Chicago, which are the three primary markets involving broadcast journalism, but it also took place in all the markets throughout the country.

The soap opera business also took a big hit. Several long-running shows including *As the World Turns*, *All My Children*, *Guiding Light* and *One Life to Live* all went off the air at that time. At 72 years, Guiding Light was the longest-running soap opera on television at the time of its cancellation, but it still couldn't survive. With the viewing audience for all the soaps dwindling, and advertisers therefore no longer willing to support the shows, the networks had to cut them loose.

Of course, the most unpredictable and earth-shattering event most people have ever experienced is the global COVID-19 pandemic. Much has been written about it and since it is ongoing, so much remains to be written. Suffice it to say that the entertainment industry has been hard hit. Almost every live theatre, concert venue and movie house were completely closed for more than a year. Production of live plays and musicals, television shows and films were stopped for months, until the industry could put safety measures in place. As a result, hundreds of thousands of people lost their jobs and according to some estimates, the entertainment industry will lose $160 billion over five years because of COVID-19.

That is simply devastating. Not only have productions suffered, so has everyone connected to them, including people I know and love the most – talent and the agents who represent them – as well as the small businesses that support them.

However, in a case of "the show must go on" the pandemic has forced people to think differently. In the case of consumers, they've had to find new ways to entertain themselves. Likewise, the entertainment industry – companies, talent, and agencies alike – has found additional ways to generate revenue. For example, streaming services such as Netflix, HBO Max and Disney+ have really taken off because people are stuck inside their homes. Video gaming has seen a rise. Theatre companies are developing completely new online offerings that will probably continue once we get past the pandemic.

There are countless other examples, which all proves that creativity finds a way to express itself.

Of course, this will cause other changes in the way the entertainment industry operates. Warner Bros. Pictures, for example, decided to simultaneously release all of its 2021 films on HBO Max and in theaters. That's good for many consumers who enjoy being entertained from the comfort and safety of their homes. But it's bad for the movie theaters, restaurants, soft drink and snack companies and everyone connected to the act of going out to see a film. In addition, streaming will cause changes in contracts for talent of all stripes, for advertisers and more.

Regardless of what the future holds for the entertainment industry, these shifts will impact American culture and media for generations to come. And if talent, agents, and businesses are not agile enough to adapt they will be left behind.

I wrote earlier about how my client Jaclyn Smith diversified herself, and in doing so, has been able to sustain a very successful career for decades.

Another example is Carl Weathers, who most famously starred as Apollo Creed opposite Sylvester Stallone in the first four *Rocky* films. I want to share a bit of Carl's story to show what diversified thinking – and having varied experiences – can do for someone.

When I met Carl, he had already had bit parts in a few television shows and films, and one huge film – *Rocky*, with Sylvester Stallone. Carl had heard about me and my reputation as a successful commercial agent, so he approached me about developing new revenue streams for himself beyond what he was doing.

In addition to his impressive physical presence, his commanding voice, and his attractive personality, the moment I met him I could tell in an instant that he was a smart, driven man. Especially when he told me some of his amazing life story.

In a rather businesslike fashion, Carl recounted how he grew up poor in New Orleans, where he fell in love with acting in grade school. Then, in the eighth grade, he diversified himself by earning an athletic scholarship to St. Augustine High School.

As Carl said, girls liked guys in football uniforms more than they did guys in tights running around spouting Shakespeare. And if you wanted to be friends with the cool guys, he said, you played sports. Although he never left his love for acting behind, at St. Augustine's, he was acclaimed for his skills as a boxer, soccer player, wrestler,

CARL WEATHERS

gymnast, and martial artist. But most of all, he was a highly talented football player.

Looking at him, and remembering all those great boxing scenes in Rocky, it was easy to see why. However, Carl again surprised me when he told me that as a teen, he also sang in bands, where he made a few extra dollars performing songs by Otis Redding, Wilson Pickett, and James Brown, among others.

While theatre, music and sports do not seem to go together, with Carl, there was a common thread – he loved the applause and approval he got when he worked hard and performed well, and he also delighted in being multi-dimensional.

After graduation from high school, he earned a football scholarship to play at San Diego State University, where he was a standout linebacker, and helped the team go undefeated and win the Pasadena Bowl. In keeping with his roots as a Renaissance Man, he did this while studying Theatre Arts. What's more, he added "singing in an a cappella group" to his repertoire, and also sang R&B in a San Diego band called "Al and the Rhythm Gents." He even released a Teddy Pendergrass-inspired single called "You Ought to Be With Me."

Let me tell you, when an imposing figure like Carl Weathers is sitting across from you and considering whether or not you should be his agent, and he shares a story about a song called, "You Ought to Be With Me," well, you do what he says.

Continuing the story, Carl talked about how he went on to play five years in the NFL, for the Oakland Raiders, and in the Canadian Football League, for the BC Lions.

He also described how, during his off seasons in the Bay Area, he attended San Francisco State University and earned a bachelor's degree in Drama. Now that's dedication.

After achieving huge success as a football player and actor – including as an acting client of mine – Carl moved to Washington State, where he started breeding and raising cattle. And, of course, he continued acting.

I can't tell you how many television shows and films he's done, but it's a lot. Most recently, a new generation of viewers can see him play Greef Karga in the *Star Wars* series *The Mandalorian*, for which he earned an Emmy nomination. In addition to his work as an actor, Carl is a director of television and film, and has directed and narrated training films for the Unites States Military.

One of the aspects of being an agent that I loved and do miss is the privilege of working with talent such as Carl – creative, gifted, driven, fiercely dedicated to the craft, and a really good guy. I feel lucky to have represented him and call him a friend. Carl appreciates how I love the arts, artists, and actors, how my heart is in the theatre, and how I take a genuine interest in people's well-being. And I appreciate how he does the same. I also place great value in him calling me a

CHANDRA WILSON

"frustrated race-car driver," which I prove every time I drive him to a Lakers game, because it makes me sound sexier than I really am.

All kidding aside, in terms of diversification, just the other day Carl said the fact that neither of us have followed a template, and have done things our way, has been a prime contributor to our success. I agree wholeheartedly.

I believe the diversity of experiences Carl has had in his life has contributed mightily to his success. If you look at his background you can see how he drew on his life experience and professional training to excel in dramatic roles, comedic roles, and action-based roles, as well as produce and direct.

From an agency perspective, having a diverse mode of thinking can lead to breakthroughs for an agent and their client that might not have been possible otherwise. For example, Richard Fisher, a senior partner and co-head of our Talent department at Abrams Artists Agency, saw an opportunity to put a client forward for a job that was not at all what the casting breakdown called for. That client was Chandra Wilson, the part was Dr. Miranda Bailey, and the show was Grey's Anatomy.

Today, viewers can't imagine anyone else in that role, which is often the case when a great actor like Chandra fully inhabits a character as she has. But when the call for auditions went out, casting directors wanted to go in a different direction. They thought her character should be, as Chandra puts it, "a petite, blonde-haired white woman with curls who was underestimated." Richard Fisher, on the other hand, knew that the show's creator, Shonda Rhimes, wanted to follow a "color-blind casting" principle while choosing the faces of her characters. He also knew Chandra wanted to stretch herself.

Chandra wowed them in her audition and got the part. Twenty-Two years later, Grey's Anatomy, and Chandra, are massive hits. Over the years, the show has received acclaim for its diverse approach to casting and for putting women of color in positions of leadership. This includes Dr. Miranda Bailey, who has gone from a resident to Chief Miranda Bailey, the leader of Grey Sloan Memorial Hospital. Further embracing the diversity principle, Chandra continues to act in films and on stage and has become an established director. And by continuing to embrace diversity and be passionate about actors and their work, Richard will no doubt create more opportunities for his clients and the agency.

Another example is producer/director/writer/actor/dancer/educator/advocate/foundation founder, Victoria Rowell. Oh, she's also a mother of two, my former client, and my good friend. As one of the most hyphenated people I've ever met, Victoria knows what it means to make diversification and agility two of her biggest strengths.

I could write an entire book about her life. But she already did! I encourage you to read her New York Times best-selling memoir, *The Women Who Raised Me.*

In the meantime, let's look at how she's prepared for and overcome a series of unpredictable events. I'm going to go into some detail here, but I think doing so will be instructive.

VICTORIA ROWELL
Photo Credit: Chris Alleyman

Victoria and her two older sisters were born in Maine and adopted by a senior-citizen widow who ran a 60-acre farm, where she spent her first 18 years. At age eight, she began to study ballet.

With help from her foster mother, she applied for and won a Ford Foundation Scholarship to study ballet in Cambridge, Massachusetts. After graduating from high school, she won another scholarship, this time to the American Ballet Theatre School, where she performed for three years – at one point, as the only black dancer there.

While she was in New York, the famed choreographer, Anthony Tudor, selected her to perform his ballet *Little Improvisation*, which was a collaboration between Juilliard, ABT, and Joffrey. Victoria also danced with Ballet Hispanico of NY and Twyla Tharp.

In one of my numerous scouting forays, I was fortunate to see Victoria dance, and of course, I was suitably impressed. Not just by her ability as a dancer, but as a potential actor for commercials. She was stunningly beautiful and had a combination of grace and determination that is uncommon in most people. And she still has those qualities. I remember walking down the street and talking with her about giving acting a try. She remembers me as being paternal and loving and sincere and smart and business like – a description I'll take any day.

Once she agreed to hang up her pointe shoes it was like she was shot out of a cannon. She modelled for Seventeen and Mademoiselle magazines and on runways. She did commercials for Ford and Levi's and Crush and a lot of other brands. Then she got a part in a film, Leonard Part 6, which led to roles on the Cosby Show and the Fresh Prince of Bel-Air. She got a part on As the World Turns.

But if all that's not enough, it was in 1990 that this young woman who was shot out of a cannon broke the sound barrier. Sometime in the prior year, black women in the south began inundating Bill Bell, the producer of CBS' hit daytime drama, *The Young and the Restless*, with mail asking for another black character. The women said they wanted to see someone that is different from Mamie Johnson, the housekeeper for the wealthy Abbott family. They loved Mamie, but they said the portrayal of Mamie wasn't painting a full and diverse picture of the black experience. They were demanding a black character be included in the show.

When I heard about this, I asked Victoria if she'd like to audition for the number one soap opera on television. She'd gotten some traction on TV and in films, and her career was headed down that path, but when I told her what the part was about, she jumped at it. Through their advocacy, the black women who had written to Bill Bell had created the role of Drucilla Winters, a runaway teen and street urchin who is taken in by Mamie, her aunt, Mamie. Over the course of her 14 years on the show, Victoria's character grows from a street-smart survivor to a ballet dancer, supermodel, mother to a rebellious teenager, and finally, major business executive.

Getting this part was a huge breakthrough for Victoria. She could hardly believe CBS was going to pay to move her and her newborn daughter from their studio apartment in New York City to a beautiful two-bedroom apartment in Los Angeles. She had to learn how to drive, and she had to buy a car for the first time in her life. Victoria will tell you today that getting that part really changed her life for the better. And not just her life, either.

Because audiences loved the Drucilla character so much, they wanted to see her family and friends, they wanted to see if she had a love interest – she did, her husband Neil Winters, played by the late actor Kristoff St. John – and they wanted to see what kind of work she did. In all, Bill Bell's hiring of Victoria inspired 12 more characters and contracts for people of color.

But wait, there's more! While she was shooting The Young and the Restless, Victoria also co-starred with Dick Van Dyke in the prime-time television series *Diagnosis: Murder* for eight seasons, appeared in 16 films, hosted the Rose Bowl and many other television specials.

In addition, I was able to negotiate an Oil of Olay commercial for Victoria that ran on *The Young and the Restless*, while she was starring in the show. This was unprecedented in the industry. In a similar fashion, I was able to get Dick Van Dyke, Victoria's co-star in Diagnosis: Murder, to appear on *The Young and the Restless*, while she was appearing in both shows.

This kind of cross-pollination illustrates why, as Victoria has said, "With my talent and Harry's business acumen, we were a match made in Heaven."

Whether they'll tell you or not, for people who have experienced bigotry, as I, a Jewish man, have, and racism, as Victoria, a black woman, has, it is not easy. And that's putting it mildly. People resented Victoria for the success she achieved, particularly, she felt, because she was a black woman. Moreover, she was willing to publicly call out the discrimination she felt she experienced on *The Young and the Restless* as well as voice her thoughts about the lack of diversity on the show, not just in front of the cameras, but also behind them.

As Victoria said during an appearance on *The Wendy Williams Show*, "It shouldn't be that way. Behind the cameras has to look like who you see in front of it." I agree wholeheartedly.

In any case, *The Young and the Restless* did what soaps often did when they wanted to get rid of an actor – they pushed her character off a cliff. Technically, the story was that Drucilla fell off a cliff during a struggle. But for all intents and purposes, the show pushed her.

Victoria and I talked a lot about what it would mean for her to take the risk of coming forward. She said she knew I had hundreds of clients, and when she stepped out, there would be repercussions. She knew she couldn't expect friends and colleagues to come along with her and commit, in her words, "entertainment suicide."

I knew what was at stake for her financially and personally. She wanted to grow in her career and grow as a person, and she didn't see why she had to separate the two. Neither did I. That's why I never stood in her way, and that's why I tried to be, as she puts it, "A balm for her soul." Today she'll tell you that, in addition to me, she's grateful to other people who championed her. People like Bill Bell, who didn't agree with what was being done to her and said, "I LOVE this girl!" And people like Fred Silverman and Paul Mason and my very close friend, Perry Simon. They all felt, as I did, that Victoria's opportunities should be limitless. Victoria agreed, of course, which is why she didn't sit around and let her anger get her down. She didn't wait for opportunities to come her. She created them for herself and others!

Here's how: She started a production company – Days Ferry Productions – to fuel her passion and give her a platform from which she can launch projects that are meaningful to her. Through her company, in 2017, Victoria created and starred in *The Rich and the Ruthless*, a six-part series that makes fun of soap operas and their lack of diversity. She created a lifestyle/decorative reality television series called *Trash vs. Treasure* which features low-income mothers improving their living spaces with found, purchased, and used items on a microbudget. She also created and starred in *Jacqueline and Jilly*, a television show about a wealthy family who has to face their daughter's addiction to painkillers. I know she's published two other books besides her memoirs, and she's produced, written, directed, and acted in several other shows, but honestly, I can't remember everything. And it's hard to keep up with her!

As we say in show business, stay tuned.

Chapter 15: Brand YOU

Master of the house, doling out the charm
Ready with a handshake and an open palm
Tells a saucy tale, makes a little stir
Customers appreciate a bon-viveur

—Alain Albert Boublil, Claude Michel
Schonberg
Herbert Kretzmer, Jean Marc Natel
From *Les Misérables*

Like it or not, you are a brand. And since every single person you encounter in life – in person and online – is a potential employer, employee or customer, you need to provide a brand experience that makes people want to hire you, work for you or buy from you.

Now, that doesn't mean everyone is going to end up in one of those categories. Most won't. But they *might*. And because they might, you must build your brand accordingly.

What does that entail?

To begin with, are you prepared and made of high quality?

By this I mean, have you gone to college or conservatory? Have you trained or interned with people who can improve you and sharpen your skills, not just once, but continually?

Have you taken on challenges that stretch your abilities and helped you grow? Have you tried and failed at something, and if so, did you learn anything from the experience?

Have you studied and immersed yourself, from every vantage point, in the subject matter of the profession you want to enter?

Have you examined who is doing what you want to do well, and who is doing it poorly?

Do you know who your competition is and how they are competing?

Have you got your references and letters of recommendation ready and gathered your testimonials? If you have worked or had internships through your college years, undergraduate and graduate, you should have asked your immediate superior or the owner of the company to write you a letter of recommendation as to what your qualities are. They can attest to your character, they can attest to your work ethic, and they can attest to your abilities in the workplace. They can talk about you in two or three or four paragraphs. Assuming you have that letter, this is the time to use it. In a similar vein, you should already have your references lined up and ready to go. Only about one or two percent of applicants have letters of recommendation and reference. It's astounding. If you don't have them, go back and ask for them to be created for you. You'll be glad you did.

Do you have your supporting materials in place so you can submit them at a moment's notice. For example, if you're an actor you need your résumé, headshot, go-to songs and monologues, and dance routines ready! If you're an employer is the "work for us" section of your website where you want it to be? If you're a company does the information you use to sell your product or service say what you want it to say?

All this and more must be thought through and put into practice before you can do anything. You can shoot from the hip and hope your charm wins the day. But 99.9 percent of the time, without these fundamentals of preparedness and quality "construction" in place, your efforts will be frustrating and fruitless.

Look at it this way: do you buy shirts that don't fit and fall apart after one wearing? Of course not. Before you spend your money you make sure the shirt is the right color and size and texture and style, and that it's made of dependable materials, don't you? Likewise, your prospective employers, employees and customers will do the same due diligence before they part with *their* money.

Next, does the way you portray yourself through your communications channels accurately reflect the image you want your brand to convey?

By this I mean, how do you come across in person and online?

Your appearance is a communication channel. Is it in line with what you're going after? For instance, if you're going to an audition for the musical *Hair*, you're not going to wear a conservative business suit. If you're interviewing for a job as a talent agent, you're not going to wear shorts and a bandana. I'm being facetious, but you'd be surprised at what I've seen people wear. And if you're selling your product to a fashion brand, you're not going to wear their competitor's brand to the appointment. Again, it may seem simple-minded to point this out, but I've heard of people making sales calls to Nike or Coca-Cola wearing Adidas and carrying Pepsi. It's not pretty.

What about Instagram, Twitter, Facebook, Tik Tok, You Tube, Linked In or your blog or web site? You may think that video of you on a boat wearing next to nothing and making out with someone while smoking a cigarette, holding a beer, and cursing into the camera is fun and shows your personality. And you may think people who care about such things when they make their hiring or buying decisions are uptight. But I assure you, no one who is going to seriously consider hiring you or buying from you, wants to see that photo — even if you want to be a fitness model or sell cigarettes and alcohol.

What I've just described is an extreme example. But I've seen and heard of far *worse*. You can use your imagination for that. I can tell you this: people who are going to part with their money in today's world are first going to closely examine how you come across online. If for no other reason, they want to know what kind of judgment you have.

People will also look at what you write online. It may feel good to write a political screed about one party or the other, and it may get you likes and followers and retweets, but it will also limit your field of opportunity to whomever supports your stance. You don't want a casting director or an author or a purchasing agent turning you down for a social or political position you're espousing. I'm not saying you should try to be someone you're not; lack of authenticity is a sure ticket to oblivion. I'm saying be mindful of what you're putting out there.

So, what kind of content should you make publicly available online?

To answer that, think of what you want your reputation to be. Said another way, for what do you want to be known? Your content, including résumé, photos, videos, writing, podcast, songs, artwork, case studies, media coverage, testimonials, product and service descriptions, and how you show up when people enter your name in search engines are all part of your brand.

And your brand reputation has a monetary value. According to an August 2018 survey by CareerBuilder, 70 percent of employers check you out on social media during the hiring process—and more than 50 percent have turned down candidates because of what they've encountered in the process. Similarly, a survey by GlobalWebIndex found that 71 percent of people are more likely to purchase products and services based on social media referrals.

I'm not advocating that you scrub everything personal and become a robot. I love my family and dogs and tennis and theatre and art and sunshine and a whole bunch of things, and I'm happy for people to know it. You should approach your interests in the same way because sharing those things makes you seem like more of a complete human being—and people want to have a sense of who you are. After all, part of their decision is whether they might want to spend time with you. Use your judgment. If you're unsure of something, delete it.

What you do in the brick-and-mortar world is also a way to communicate about your brand attributes. For example, my personal brand indicates I'm a big supporter of performing artists, and always will be. That's conveyed by philanthropic activities I'm involved in that reflect those attributes. In Victoria Rowell's case, she started and runs a foundation that helps foster children. Neither of us do these things because we think it will make us look good—we do them because we feel passionate about them. The fact that those activities say something about our personal brands is incidental.

Another way to send a message about your brand identity is networking. Said another way, with whom do you associate? If you write books or plays or screenplays, do you belong to the Authors Guild, Dramatists Guild or Writers Guild, and do you go to their events? If you're an agent, do you go to literary conferences or drama schools or film festivals? If you're an entrepreneur, do you go to places where investors and other entrepreneurs hang out? If you not only belong to groups such as these, and attend their events, but are also actively participating by lecturing or hosting or sponsoring things than you are creating deeper bonds with people. And by enabling people to create deeper bonds with you, you are helping them have a more complete experience with your brand.

Now let's talk about the communications outreach that's necessary to get a job.

Getting a job now is different than when I started out. As I said earlier, over the course of my career the internet, email, web sites, cell phones, social media, cell phone apps, texting, networking opportunities and more have all completely changed the way business is done. That's true whether you're in the entertainment industry or not.

But some fundamentals never change. Namely, communicating with prospective employers and customers – who you are, what you want to do, and why you're the best person to do it. Not just once, but continuously. It's the *how* that's changed.

I don't want to sound like a curmudgeon or oversimplify the topic but as the distribution channels for communicating have proliferated, I've seen a dramatic divergence in the skill at which people use those channels. And that gap in skill can be the main difference between launching a career or staying on the launch platform.

Let's start with the basics – how you introduce yourself to a prospective employer in a letter or email.

I know what you're thinking. Do people even read these things anymore? Can't they just look at my résumé? Anyway, it's who you know, right?

Believe me, people read these letters and emails. Now, if you're on the talent side of the entertainment industry writing and applying for a job is not how it's done. But if you want almost any other kind of professional job you need to correspond professionally. Put yourself in the shoes of a human resources screener or a hiring manager. They see résumé after résumé, and often encounter people who don't even take the time to write a letter or email. Or if they do write something, it's terrible. For example, I've seen correspondence that says only, "see résumé," thinking that will suffice. It will not. Instead, you want to use your outreach as an opportunity to expand upon your résumé, give your prospective employer a tangible example of your communication skill, tell them who you are in an engaging way, highlight specific information about your experience that directly addresses what the hiring manager is looking for – in other words – how you can solve their problem – and rise above other candidates.

There are a lot of resources you can look to for advice. In my experience, here are a few basics that will help you stand out.

First, before you begin writing, research everything you can about the company. Find out who is in what jobs. Read news articles about them. If they have an annual report, study it. Learn what they say their challenges are and what they're proud of. Watch videos of their people giving speeches. It's all important.

Second, don't recycle old letters and emails, replacing the prior company you targeted with the new one. Employers will see right through that and think you simply don't care enough to try. Write something new for each position, even if you're applying to more than one position within the same company. If you customize your outreach to address needs hiring managers have specifically cited, you will get their attention. Why? Because most people don't.

Third, do not be generic and use "Dear Sir/Madam" or "To Whom It May Concern." Do your homework. Find out who it is and use their name. If you don't use the person's name, they'll think you don't care enough to try. Are you seeing a pattern here? Conversely, do not be so informal that you act as if you're old pals when you don't even know the person. I can't tell you how many times I've seen and immediately discarded communications that begin, "Hi Harry!" or "Hiya Harry!" or even "Hey Harry." You think I'm joking. I'm not. Worse than that are people who write like they're texting their friends and don't bother to capitalize or use punctuation, writing, "hi" or "hi harry" or even "hey man." If any one of those people had done a modicum of research, they would have discovered they should write, "Dear Mr. Abrams." Different companies and industries prefer different approaches. For the love of God, find out what it is and use it.

Fourth, write in an active voice. If I wrote that sentence in a passive voice it would say something like this, "the writing should be done in an active manner."

150

Fifth, open and close strong. You don't have to tell me your name and where you live. The hiring manager can see that, hopefully, on your résumé. And don't try to be too clever or funny. The person you're writing to wants to know what position you're applying for, why you're passionate about the company and position, what you have to offer, some of your accomplishments, what you might do with the position, and end with a call to action. I'm not saying do all of that in one opening and closing sentence. I'm saying those are all the elements you need, and the sooner you get to them and through them the better off you'll be.

Finally, run your letter or email through spell check and grammar check. Share it with a few people you trust and ask for their feedback. And don't be defensive when receiving it.

Once you've had your interview, you should always follow it up with a thank you letter or email. Believe it or not, most people do not do that. Again, put yourself in the interviewer's shoes. Their time is valuable. They are taking time out of their busy day to see you. They may have seen 10 people that day, 10 the day before, and 10 the day before that. And they're going to see 10 people tomorrow. How do you expect them to remember you? They do it by promptly getting a well-written note of appreciation and thanks. In that note, you reference some of the things that were discussed at the interview. You bring up items you wish you had said but couldn't because you ran out of time. Don't rehash the entire interview. But do say enough to leave a lasting impression.

All the communications tactics I've cited are the things you need to build and nurture your brand when you're looking for a job — whether you're just starting out or already a veteran. You can apply these practices to starting and growing a business, too. And if you're on the talent side of the business it's a whole different culture and approach than what I've just described. If you've studied your craft in college or conservatory or through some other training, or you've got an agent or manager or even a mentor, you've probably already learned what to do. If you haven't, you need to do the research, find a class, and get started.

Chapter 16: The Business of YOU

There is a tide in the affairs of men.
Which, taken at the flood, leads on to fortune;
Omitted, all the voyage of their life
Is bound in shallows and in miseries.
On such a full sea are we now afloat,
And we must take the current when it serves,
Or lose our ventures.

—William Shakespeare
From *Julius Caesar*

Right away, I know the title of this chapter will be an insult to the types of talent I represented in my career. "I'm not in business, I'm an ARTIST!"

Yes, you are. But you must also look at yourself as an entrepreneur who is starting and running a business. And the business is you.

As the CEO of YOU, Inc., you are the product and service, and you are also the head of sales, marketing, communications, manufacturing, legal, human resources, finance, supply chain, distribution, research and development, and every other department in a business.

That's right, as talented an artist as you may be, you are Apple, ExxonMobil and Walmart.

"But wait," you say. "I studied acting at RADA and Juilliard. I trained as a playwright and screenwriter at the Yale School of Drama. I have a degree in directing from NYU. I didn't go to Harvard or

Wharton to study business and work on Wall Street. That's for. . .other people."

Then, for good measure, you add a sniff and a hair toss and proclaim, "I'm not a sellout!"

No, you're not. But let me ask you this: Would you like to be the world's finest talent and be home sitting on the couch eating ramen noodles and wondering how you're going to pay your rent, or would you rather be the world's finest talent and feel relatively secure that you can eat well and pay your bills because you are working so much?

If you were in the second category, I wanted to work with you. If you were in the first category, I wanted you to understand that you had much in common with business, and if you started thinking and acting that way, I would want to work with you.

Many of the people I encountered when they were just getting out of school, and this includes artists and prospective agents, thought getting a degree would somehow magically open doors and suitors would be lining up to hire them. When casting directors and producers and agencies weren't hiring them, and didn't even know they existed, it was a rude awakening.

Perhaps they were told they'd be taught business management in their performing arts school, and maybe someone came in and gave a one-hour lecture on the topic one day. Having provided this extensive education, the school could tell themselves they had properly prepared their performing arts students for the real world of show business. And the students could go away secure in the knowledge that they knew what to do when they got out.

But what really happened was students left school with an unrealistic sense of their own marketability and vaguely thought, regarding the business side of things, "I'll have someone else handle that. Like an agent or a business manager. I'll just focus on being an artist."

Well, if you and I were to sit down at lunch and you asked for my advice on how to launch and build your career, the following is what I would tell you.

You are an entrepreneur, and no one has taught you how to be one. It's okay, but that's the truth. I am meeting you where you are, and together, we will look forward.

For starters, you must embark on a course of self-study, read everything you can find on the business of your art, and listen to people who are doing what you want to do. Go to lectures, watch videos, meet people in person and ask them questions. Talk to entrepreneurs and ask for their advice. In business, this function is called "learning and development." With an attitude of lifelong learning, get started now, and never stop. Take inspiration from the great cellist, Pablo Casals, who, when he was in his 80s, was asked why he continued to practice the cello four and five hours a day, and answered, "Because I think I am making progress."

As you discover things about being an entrepreneur, try putting them into practice. Don't wait until you think you know everything. No one will ever know everything. Try and fail and learn. What do you have to lose?

One thing you can try right away is creating your own work.

While I discovered more than a few talents in my career, sometimes in unlikely places – parks, shopping malls, talent competitions – artists cannot depend on luck. You can't wait for someone to happen by. There are too many people vying for attention these days and there is too little time to see everyone. What you need to do is create something out of nothing. Write a scene for a play or screenplay. Put on a show. Create a cabaret act. Film something. Write and record a song. Get a friend and go perform a pas de deux at a community center. Whatever your art form is, use it to make a piece of art. Get as many people as possible to see it. If you can make money doing it, great. If not, at least you're putting yourself and your work out there. And while you're at it, ask other artists to do it with you. You're all in the same boat. You create an opportunity for someone now, maybe they'll create one for you later.

One famous example of creating your own work is Sylvester Stallone. He wanted to act. So, what did he do? Did he wait for an agent or casting director to discover him? Did he shake his fist at people on the sidewalk and whine about not getting noticed? Who knows? But I'll tell you what he did do: he wrote a screenplay called *Rocky* and told studios he wasn't going to sell it to them unless he could star in it. He was a nobody at the time. Look at him now.

Another example is Rob McElhenny. At the age of 27, while waiting tables in Los Angeles, McElhenny met Glenn Howerton and Charlie Day, told them about an idea he had for a sitcom, spent a total of $200 to film it, pitched it to cable networks, and sold it to FX. That show is the comedy series *It's Always Sunny in Philadelphia*, which is now in its 16th season.

There are many other examples, but I'll give you one more, from the world of publishing. Long before she wrote *The Handmaid's Tale* and saw her book turned into a series for Hulu, Canadian author, Margaret Atwood self-published an award-winning book of poems called *Double Persephone*. I'd say she got herself noticed.

Another thing you must do is vigorously market your product — which is you. You can have the best product in the world, but if no one knows about it no one is going to buy it. It's up to you to get yourself noticed and keep yourself in front of potential buyers.

For example, in business, the computer science geniuses at IBM's labs created the best operating system in the industry but they were beaten in the marketplace by a competitor with an inferior product but a far superior marketing campaign — Microsoft. While IBM was trying to be "pure" and make a flawless operating system, Microsoft was making theirs just good enough to sell. And when they found weaknesses in their product, they fixed them and treated the fixes as new and improved versions, thus creating a new marketing opportunity — and billions upon billions of dollars of revenue.

If you're an actor without a marketing budget like Microsoft's, what do you do? You contact people in the industry. Write to agents and producers and casting directors. Talk your way into directors' screenings. Go to open auditions. Get people's business cards. Record a monologue or a song or a dance and post it to social media. Write an article for your local newspaper. Start a blog or podcast. Get on other people's podcasts. If you're performing in something, let people know about it. Even after it's over, tell people you were in it; people who can hire you want to know that you're not just sitting around. You're busy working, taking classes, performing.

It's like in business, if you're employed, people want to hire you, but if you're unemployed, they don't. It's counterintuitive, but that's how it is.

You know the music industry mogul, Jay Z? No record label would touch him when he was just starting out. What did he do? He sold CDs out of his car until he could make enough money and contacts to start his own record label and produce his first album, *Reasonable Doubt*. *Rolling Stone* magazine called it one of the 500 best albums of all time. Without Jay Z willing it to happen we may never have heard of him.

When you're an entrepreneur you never stop looking for opportunities to market yourself. Even when you're famous. Even when you are over 80 years old. Like Sir Patrick Stewart, an iconic star of stage and screen and a classically trained actor. He has more than 3.6 million followers on Twitter, 1.6 million on Instagram, and 6 million on Facebook. And he even has more than 12,000 followers on TikTok, which is skewed to people who are five or six decades younger than him. When @SirPatStew, as he calls himself, realized people were getting increasingly anxious during the coronavirus pandemic, including himself, he looked for a way to use his skills to distract and calm them. He started recording himself reading William Shakespeare's sonnets, and then he posted the recordings to his social media accounts. They were wildly popular.

As you can see from Sir Patrick Stewart's example, marketing doesn't have to be "unseemly" or "beneath you." In fact, it must be in keeping with your personal brand.

In the case of young clients like Dove Cameron and Jordan Fisher, we advised them to build their presence on social media channels such as Facebook, Instagram, Twitter, Snapchat, TikTok and YouTube. That's because many networks, studios and advertisers in the past few years have become less interested in casting or hiring performers who have acting training or important theatre and film credits, and instead want to know how many thousands or millions of social media "followers" they have.

Also, you don't have to be famous to keep yourself in the public eye. In fact, there's a guy who calls himself "The Ghost" who gained more than 1.2 million Instagram followers in six months despite never revealing his face, name, talent or occupation. If someone who wears a bedazzled ski mask over his face can go from unknown to well-known without showcasing any particular skills or knowledge surely you can market yourself.

Here's another aspect of business that is so obvious I almost hesitate to state it: get comfortable with selling. As a performer, you already know how to listen to your audience. You can sense what other people are feeling, especially your fellow performers. If you're good, you are generous and give others a chance to shine. Also, you find the truth in every character you play. You know if you give a false performance, your scene partner and your audience will know. The same goes for selling. If you're lying, your customer will know or soon find out. So many of the same qualities that make you a good performer will also make you a good salesperson.

One way to develop your skills is to work as an actual salesperson. Do that and you get to practice your acting and make money at the same time. Johnny Depp, for example, sold ballpoint pens over the phone and considered it to be his first experience with acting. George Clooney sold women's shoes and was a door-to-door life insurance salesman. Kanye West worked at a retail store selling clothes. Ellen DeGeneres sold vacuum cleaners. Clint Black sold newspaper subscriptions door-to-door, which he has in common with me!

I cannot overstate how important selling is. As an artist, you must be able to sell your ideas to people who have the ability, and money, to bring your ideas to life. To me, the ultimate person in this regard was William Shakespeare. Besides being history's greatest playwright and storyteller, he was an actor, producer, theatre company owner, and real estate investor. While we imagine producers automatically buying his plays due to their sheer brilliance, you know he had to make a case for them. In other words, he had to sell them.

If Shakespeare could do it, so can you. Again, you don't have be famous to do it. Consider the Brazilian author, Paulo Coelho. Virtually unknown, he sold his book, *The Alchemist*, to an obscure Brazilian publisher. They printed a mere 900 copies. After a year of very poor sales the publisher returned the rights to Coelho. Disappointed but undaunted because he believed so strongly in his work, Coelho started knocking on doors to sell the book. Another publisher picked up the book. To make a long story short, Paulo Coelho has now sold more than 350 million books in 150 countries. *The Alchemist* has been on *The New*

York Times bestseller list for more than 315 weeks. It has also been translated into 80 different languages, setting the Guinness World Record for the most translated book by any living author. And this success may not have ever happened unless Coelho believed in his work and was comfortable selling it.

Another key aspect of business is financing, which I know makes artists break out in a sweat when they think about it. But really, you must become good at raising money to support the projects you want to create. You've heard of startup businesses "bootstrapping," getting "seed capital" and "early-stage financing" from "angel investors" and venture capitalists so they can "go public?" You don't need all those terms, but you do need money to do what you want to do. When you're just starting out, you're likely to get money from friends and family, from your own savings, from loans, from credit cards, from home mortgages, and so on. You get people to work for free, or for next to nothing. You get someone to supply the food. You produce your project at a friend's house. Whatever it takes. If you believe in it enough, you'll do anything to raise the money and create your project. In the last few years, digital technology has made it possible for artists to easily and quickly raise large sums of money to produce their projects. There's no reason you can't do it, too.

In addition to everything I've described so far, one of the most important qualities you need to succeed in business is resilience. This is true whether you're an artist, agent, or an entrepreneur. In fact, even if you haven't worked a day in your life, you will experience adversity, rejection, and self-doubt. Everyone wants something at some point in their lives, and everyone has experienced the pain and disappointment of not getting it. How you respond to these setbacks is what's important.

To that end, I would like to hire and work with people with good pedigrees and training, including straight-A graduates from top universities and conservatories, people who trained or worked with other high-quality professionals, and those who excelled at prior positions. Who wouldn't?

But I'll tell you what: I'd rather work with someone who was a C student, worked their way through college, and tried and failed in a few ventures but never gave up, emerged stronger each time, and was willing to do what it took to succeed. Whereas the first person may feel a sense of entitlement, the second person uses adversity as a chance to build resilience. To the second person, resilience is the foundation for everything else I've talked about: seeing yourself as the CEO of your life, being a lifelong learner, creating your own work, marketing yourself, getting comfortable with selling, and raising money. That's how valuable resilience is.

Look, as much as I love the entertainment industry, being an entrepreneur, and being a talent agent, and as grateful as I am for the experiences I've had because of those things, they can all break your heart – if you let them.

Don't let them.

In this regard, I think of my friend and former client, the two-time Emmy winning television, film and theatre actor, Michael Emerson. Before he played roles such as William Hinks on *The Practice*, Benjamin Linus on *Lost*, Zep Hindle in *Saw*, Cayden James on *Arrow*, Harold Finch on *Person of Interest*, and Dr. Leland Townsend on *Evil*, he spent a long time, in his words, "without a pot to pee in." Unable to find acting work in New York, he took retail jobs, worked as an illustrator and teacher, appeared in local theatre productions in Jacksonville, and went back to school to get a Master of Fine Arts at the University of Alabama in the Alabama Shakespeare Festival. He was 43 years old before he landed the starring role as Oscar Wilde in the critically acclaimed off-Broadway play *Gross Indecency: The Three Trials of Oscar Wilde*. Since that breakthrough, he's never been out of work as an actor, and has built an impressive career. Richard Fisher, one of our outstanding theatrical agents, has been his champion in building a career with Michael.

Another one of our clients that I think of in this regard is the actress, Kerry Washington. Long before she landed the lead role on Shonda Rhimes' *Scandal*, Kerry said, in a conversation with *The Hollywood Reporter*, that she had been part of two pilots—the shows were picked up but she was replaced. The two failures broke her heart—and lit a fire under her. To ground herself, she went back to her roots – "to the wilderness" – and did a Broadway play called *Race*. She credits the experience with helping her find her path and find success on the acclaimed television show for which is she's known. "Going into

Michael Emerson

the wilderness made me ready — as an artist, as a person, as a businesswoman — to receive *Scandal*," she said.

In the early 1990s, Jennifer Lopez was a backup dancer for New Kids on the Block, and a Fly Girl on Fox's *In Living Color,* when I signed her as a client. Today, Jennifer is an actress, businesswoman, producer, singer, model and dancer who has performed on two of the world's biggest stages – the NFL Super Bowl Halftime Show, and the inauguration of President Joe Biden – and is one of the most powerful women in entertainment. Growing up in the tough Castle Hill section of the Bronx, the daughter of poor parents from Puerto Rico, was not easy. "Jenny from the block" faced a lot of doubt and criticism and adversity on her way to becoming the superstar she is today. She told *GQ* magazine, "Because I was Latin, and I was a woman, and I was Puerto Rican, they were not giving me the same pass that they gave everybody else at certain times." Instead of letting her critics get her down she focused on getting better and told herself, "Just be resilient. They'll give up."

Forbes magazine has an excellent article on this topic. In it, 10 members of the Young Entrepreneur Council shared their experiences and insights on how to handle adversity with grace. Their tips included learning from the failures of others; being honest with yourself; building confidence and expertise by stretching beyond what you thought possible; not taking things personal; doing the work that's in front of you instead of projecting into the future; surrounding yourself with positive people who will support you; having a grand vision and purpose that's bigger than just you; continually developing your skills; expecting adversity and failure without taking them to heart.

Chapter 17: Putting it Together

Bit by bit
Putting it together
Piece by piece
Only way to make a work of art
Every moment makes a contribution
Every little detail plays a part
Having just a vision's no solution
Everything depends on execution
Putting it together
That's what counts

—Stephen Sondheim
From *Sunday in the Park with George*

At the beginning of Stephen Sondheim and James Lapine's fantastic musical, *Sunday in the Park with George*, the painter Georges Seurat is sitting among a group of Parisians at a park on the River Seine. While drawing sketches of a work he wants to begin he says, "White, a blank page or canvas. The challenge: bring order to the whole, through design, composition, tension, balance, light, and harmony." As he describes what he is drawing more people come on stage to fill up the canvas he is imagining in his head. Then, the setting suddenly changes to a gallery where the completed painting is being shown. Viewing the painting, the critics, including his fellow artists, all of whom will one day be forgotten as inconsequential, put down George's work.

This book is about what takes place between the metaphorical blank canvas and the fully realized masterpiece that is your life and work.

In his painting, Seurat, along with Paul Signac, branched from Impressionism to invent a style that art critics of the late 1880s called "Pointillism." In the technique, Seurat, Signac, Van Gogh, Pissarro, and other contemporaries applied patterns of tiny, distinct dots of color to the canvas to produce complete images. This was a new, innovative, and risky method of painting that grew out of Seurat's and Signac's fertile imaginations. They were offering something unique to the world, and critics, just as they had when they ridiculed earlier Impressionists for breaking with convention and creating *their* new style, were having none of it.

Similarly, during the first run of *Sunday in the Park with George* on Broadway, audience members routinely walked out. And while the show had its champions in the media, including Frank Rich from the *New York Times*, most of the reviews were negative. It won only two Tony Awards, for set design and lighting. And despite winning the 1985 Pulitzer Prize for Drama, the show closed at a financial loss.

But look who got the last laugh. Seurat's brilliance is now unquestioned. And the musical, which has twice been revived on Broadway, is slated for another run in London.

Seurat's painting, *A Sunday Afternoon on the Island of La Grande Jatte—1884*, and the musical it inspired, resonate deeply with me. For one thing, I love and collect fine art, and I love and "collect" – by virtue of seeing as many productions as possible – fine theatre.

I also appreciate how Seurat bucked convention and did things his way, as has Sondheim. In my life, I've done the same. Several of my friends, when interviewed for this book, said they always admired that I did things my way. From the beginning.

For instance, my father told me to get a job delivering newspapers, but I created a business selling newspapers and hiring others to sell them for me.

My mother wanted me to be an actor, but I became a person who represented them.

My parents wanted me to go to medical school, but I studied business.

When the lawn mower company tried to keep me by giving me more money, I took a job in entertainment that paid 85 percent less.

When MCA broke up, I could have stayed with the company in production, but I opened my own business instead.

Noel Rubaloff told me not to expand our agency and go to New York, but I did it anyway.

When CAA offered me a leadership position after Noel fired me, I turned it down and rebuilt my own agency – from scratch.

When my company repeatedly could have been acquired or acquired others, I grew organically.

When I could have hired high-priced, already-established agents from other companies, I decided to train and promote from within.

Other agencies splashed their names and their agents' names all over the news whenever their clients had success, but I stayed in the background and put my clients in the spotlight.

While the big corporate agencies looked at their clientele as cogs in their churning wheel of profit, and hardly saw them after signing them, I looked at my clients as part of our family, welcomed them to my home, personally went to see them wherever they were performing, took them to Lakers games and the theatre with me, and cheered on their every success.

The biggest agencies stabbed each other in the back, stole each other's clients, treated their talent as commodities, and fought to the death over the top four or five spots in the agency rankings. But I was content to grow, slowly but surely, staying in the top 10 talent agencies each year, by focusing on our clients and employees, helping both grow their lives and careers.

And when a lot of people in my position sold out, took the money, and ran to retirement, I kept working at it – not because I needed the money, but because I loved it. Like the aforementioned shark.

Sure, I ultimately sold my company – when I was in my early 80s. Why did I stay in the game so long? I loved it like I love my family. To me, work and life were intertwined. In fact, they still are as I am at this very moment writing a book about my life and how I hope my experience can help other people.

I must admit that my altruism was not always at the front of my mind. Said another way, it was not always the initial reason for doing some of the things I did in the way that I did them. I was first and foremost an entrepreneur, and a CEO, and I was about building and sustaining a profitable and growing business. It took me a while to figure out that I could do well and do good at the same time. That my business could be profitable while helping people and the planet. Let me restate that: I was slow to realize that we could be profitable *because* we were helping people and the planet.

Although I came to this realization gradually, it was one of my employees, Marni Rosenzweig, who really opened my eyes to what was possible. I'm proud of many of my past employees, but I want to talk about Marni because her career trajectory and the way she has lived her life is integrated in a way that elevates and complements both.

After graduating with honors from UCLA in 1996, where she earned a Bachelor of Arts degree in Political Science, Marni joined Abrams Artists Agency in our agent in training program. Over the next two decades, her unwavering passion, dedication and leadership qualities fueled her rise from promising mailroom employee to senior vice president and head of Talent at the company.

In early 2012, Marni realized her vision of creating a philanthropic organization within the agency that would foster collaboration between our various departments and inspire people to do good for the community at large. Marni's witty husband, Greg Rosenzweig, gave it a name, "Agents of Change," and the small but mighty team made great strides during her tenure, partnering with various organizations such as Habitat for Humanity, Heal the Bay and the Greater West Hollywood Food Coalition.

I'll never forget hearing Marni speak to our employees at the wrap-up event for the first year of Agents of Change. I was bursting my buttons with pride as I watched this young woman recount why Agents of Change was started and talk about all that had been done while giving credit to everyone else but herself. This young woman that we'd hired for the mailroom had grown her leadership abilities to such an extent that *she* was now influencing *me*.

When she first came to me with the idea for Agents of Change, in 2012, I told her she could do it "as long as it didn't cost the agency anything, and as long as it wasn't during working hours." Not exactly a ringing endorsement and a truckload of support from someone she looked up to – me.

At that wrap up party, I listened, and learned. By the end, I wiped my eyes in appreciation, humility, and gratitude.

I thought back to the first Agents of Change event I attended. It was the Heal the Bay event at Santa Monica beach. Now, often at events such as this in and around Los Angeles, the people who show up include many, if not mostly, rich, ego-driven, perfectly coiffed, surgically enhanced "beautiful people" looking at their watches and at each other to see who's there, especially from the media, and where the best spots might be to upstage one another.

This event bore no resemblance to that. As soon as I arrived, I was given a pair of rubber gloves and put to work picking up trash from the beach. Given my experience picking up paper clips from the office carpet, this was a task for which I was eminently qualified.

The group that day consisted of people at all levels of the organization working side-by-side. It wasn't senior management in their own group, separate from the rest, patting each other on the back over how wonderful *they* were. It was people from the mailroom and agents and department heads and partners all bent at the waste, picking up nasty garbage, right next to each other.

When I was pulling this kind of duty in the U.S. Army, the sergeants barked at us, "All I wanna see are asses and elbows! Get to work and don't stop until I tell ya!" But at the Santa Monica beach that day it was nothing but love and encouragement and the shared sacrifice of a few hours to help other people, and in this case, the planet.

By the time I sold the agency a steadily growing group of volunteers were participating in about one Agents of Change event per month. If you were in the mailroom or the agent-in-training program you wanted to be there because that's where the senior leaders were. That's just smart business. Agents of Change also impacted our hiring. We became known for what we were doing to the extent that job candidates routinely and proactively cited Agents of Change as one of the reasons they were interested in joining our company. So, too, did the talent we represented and the talent we wanted to sign. None of these benefits were the impetus for starting Agents of Change, but they were indeed the result.

Although Agents of Change was small in terms of what we could contribute compared to large agencies such as CAA, WME, UTA and ICM, but it was huge in the significance it played at Abrams Artists Agency in our shared experience of community and giving. I thank Marni and Sharon Paz, one of our other theatrical agents dedicated to advancing Agents of Change, for helping me see the light.

Much has been written about the "triple bottom line" of people, planet and profits, including by John Elkington, who coined the term in 1994. More recently, Rajendra Sisdodia, a professor at Babson, a school well-known for its program in entrepreneurial studies, co-write a book, with Whole Foods CEO, John Mackey, called Conscious Capitalism which describe businesses that serve the interests of all the major stakeholders of every company: communities, customers, employees, the environment, suppliers—and investors.

Leaders who embrace these ideas will tell you that by keeping *all* of those stakeholders in mind, it allows them to focus on a higher purpose than simply making a profit. In addition, Sisdodia's research shows that brands following the principles of conscious capitalism returned 1,025 percent during his decade-long study. The S&P 500 yielded 316 percent during the same time. In other words, conscious capitalism companies did more than three times as well.

But as I said earlier, the benefits of this approach to doing business extend far beyond financial return.

No one in my career ever told me that doing well by doing good would help my business. Or that I'd benefit as a person. That's not to say I didn't do very well and didn't do a lot of good. I did both, and I reaped the rewards. But I didn't connect my efforts. I achieved strong financial returns because I was running a business. And I contributed to causes that were largely related to the entertainment industry because I loved it – especially the talented artists who were making art.

To that end, my friend Arvin Brown, two-time Tony-award winner and former long-time artistic director of the Long Wharf Theatre in New Haven, Connecticut, recently talked about what lessons he thinks can be drawn from my life and work. He said, "It's clear Harry has always had successful business instincts. It's also clear that those instincts are based on his genuine love of talent. From the moment I met him, I was impressed with Harry's sense of class and enthusiasm. He has a genuine excitement, not just for his clients, but for everyone doing great work. This was obvious from the way his clients felt toward him, and the way people who weren't even his clients treated him with reverence when they saw him. Everyone knew he appreciated the work and the people doing it, even if he didn't take any credit for it. For example, I often worked with Harry's clients in theatre, television, and films – without even knowing it. He would show up on a set, and I'd wonder what he was doing there, until one of my actors would literally run to greet him. There is no dividing line between him doing well and doing good. That's just who he is."

I met Arvin through his niece, the casting director Deborah Brown, who introduced us. She knew Arvin and I both loved theatre and the artists who make theatre, and that we would hit it off. In fact, today she says the friendship between us is the "best she's ever cast." I'm also good friends with her. Not only did she cast many of my clients – including Tony Heald, Jason Alexander, and David Strathairn – she has gone to the theatre with me dozens of times over the past four decades. She jokes that, given my habit of dozing off during performances, she's been "sleeping with me for 40 years." She, like Arvin, appreciate the need to combine art with business.

When I think of good examples of putting the total package of life and work together, my friend Eric Falkenstein, a theatre, film, and television producer, comes to mind. Winner of seven Tony Awards, Eric has produced dozens of Broadway shows including *Network*; *Moulin Rouge*; *To Kill a Mockingbird*; *The Sound Inside*; *Hello, Dolly*; *The Crucible*; *All My Sons*; *The Iceman Cometh*; *Fiddler on the Roof*; *Ragtime*; *The Color Purple*; *Long Day's Journey Into Night*; *Present Laughter*; *The Wavery Gallery*; *The History Boys*; *The Miracle Worker*; *Thurgood*; and many others. Thanks to my friendship with Eric, I've been fortunate to see most of those shows.

If Broadway's not enough to snap your head back, Eric has also produced several films, including *Butler*, directed by Lee Daniels, and starring Oprah Winfrey.

While that list of accomplishments is impressive, it's just one side of the ledger.

Eric's projects are often multi-year endeavors, so when he takes one on, beyond his substantial financial commitment, his heart has to be in it. With that in mind, he says, "I look for plays I think will appeal to today's audience, have something to say, and speak to a social issue."

An example of how he applies that filter to the choices he makes is a two-part epic about Martin Luther King Jr. and the Civil Rights Movement that he's been trying to bring to the stage. Remembering the impact seeing *Eyes on the Prize* had on him many years earlier, Eric wrote the Martin Luther King Jr. play himself along with the late Congressman John R. Lewis. Eric is also working on the project with Andrew Young, the politician, diplomat and activist, who has become his dear friend.

When it comes to looking for plays that make it through his filter of having current appeal, an important message, and social impact, Eric's play is a perfect vehicle. The story of how Eric got to this point – successful producer and playwright – illustrates the choices one must make in putting their life and work together.

After growing up in the wealthy suburbs of Connecticut, and attending an exclusive private school, Eric studied sociology at Haverford College. His choice of Haverford, with its focus on civil rights, human rights, and the environment, was an early indication of where his interests lie. He next attended Yale Law School, and upon graduating, took the traditional route of working for a prominent law firm. Although his firm let him do pro bono work on the causes he cared about, they naturally wanted more from him; in the legal field you either make partner or you move on. Eric followed his heart and moved on, starting his own theatrical production company, Sparks Productions.

I can honestly say Eric's work in theatre and films is making a difference in the world. Whenever I leave one of his productions I am moved deeply inside. And although I might not show it, I am thinking about the message I just received. In the hands of people like Eric, and many of the wonderful artists with whom I've had the privilege to work, theatre is a transcendent gift to humanity.

Since 2003, when I first met Eric after his Broadway production of *Long Day's Journey Into Night*, we've often talked about the challenges of developing and mounting Broadway productions, juggling a professional and personal schedule, balancing the needs of work and life, and the importance and value of trying to be a good husband and parent. When I was his age, I didn't give it as much thought as I should have. Eric does, and it shows.

Another friend of mine, Gary Zuckerbrod, a former TV network executive, President of the Casting Society of America, and casting director for more than 35 years, often gives back by teaching young talent how to navigate the business. About me, he has said, "Harry understands what actors do, not as commodities, but as artists. He also knows that acting is a business, and because of that, actors are the CEOs of all aspects of their lives. Integrating your life and work in that fashion, as Harry has done, and as I try to do, makes both aspects that much richer."

Gary, who also serves on the Western Council of the Actors Fund, shared a story from the organization's 125th anniversary that illustrates the interdependence between acting and business. He said in the 1880s actors would go from town to town in wagons to perform for paying audiences. When they arrived at a location, the town would keep the nut that held the wagon wheel together until the actors could make enough money to pay them to get the nut back. This was how the term "making my nut" came into being. Given that the Actors Fund helps actors gain financial literacy, as I stated earlier, this story makes perfect sense. Gary is a good friend and embodies the "do well, do good" philosophy in everything he does.

Finally, I must talk about an organization that is near and dear to my heart – The Music Center in Los Angeles, where I was a founding member of the board of directors for the Fraternity of Friends fundraising group. As downtown LA's cultural destination and home to four renowned resident companies—Center Theatre Group, Los Angeles Master Chorale, LA Opera and LA Phil—The Music Center convenes artists, communities, and ideas with the goal of deepening the cultural lives of every resident in Los Angeles County.

While serving at The Music Center I began to actively participate in their annual *Spotlight* program – now in its 33rd year – a free nationally acclaimed arts training and scholarship program for Southern California teens. *Spotlight* awards Grand Prizes to two finalists in each of seven categories: acting, ballet, dance, classical voice, non-classical voice, classical instrumental and jazz instrumental. In addition to performing in the finale event, each student receives a $5,000 scholarship. The Music Center also names an Honorable Mention in each category, awarding each student with a $1,000 scholarship.

I had been mentoring and coaching young artists in the program for about 15 years when I met Jeri Gaile, a former actress on *Dallas*, *Murder She Wrote*, and *Night Court*, and dancer with American Ballet Theatre, who took over running the *Spotlight* program. As an artist in her own right, and someone who not only transferred her skills to transition to a more administration management role but also taught others the same, Jeri was, and is, the perfect person for the job.

It was through *Spotlight* that I came to know and work with artists like Erin Mackey, star of Broadway's *Wicked, Sondheim on Sondheim, Anything Goes, Chaplin,* and *Amazing Grace;* Misty Copeland, who made history in the dance world as the first African American principal dancer for American Ballet Theatre; Adam Lambert and Josh Groban, Grammy-nominated recording artists; Kris Bowers, Emmy Award-winning and Academy Award-nominated composer whose work includes the scores for *Bridgerton, Green Book* and *Dear White People;* Lindsay Mendez, Tony Award winner for her role in the Broadway revival of *Carousel* and now starring in CBS's television drama *All Rise;* and many others.

The impact of *Spotlight* on my life, and the lives of so many others, is immeasurable. Jeri described it best when she said, "*Spotlight* is a tight knit family and community where the adults support the participants, and the kids themselves root and pull for each other. Performing in front of others and being critiqued, especially by highly recognized experts, is not an easy thing to do, but we create a nurturing and empowering environment for kids to believe in themselves, because we believe in them." Josh Groban made a special appearance in last year's virtual Grand Finale performance, and we were thrilled to have him host the show this year. We know it means a lot to the kids to see *Spotlight* alumni come back to support the program, and he set the perfect example that dreams really can come true."

I could go on and on about the organizations and people to whom I've made contributions of time and money and support, and about friends and colleagues who have done the same. But that's not my goal here.

What I want to do is say this: Your life and your career are your creation, and they belong together. You don't have a life on the one hand, and a career on the other. You have a life, period, and it is a work of art.

When you're up close to your life and career you may not be able to connect the dots that comprise it, or even see the dots, as in the case of pointillism, until you take a step back. That's when the full picture comes into view, as it is with me now. My hope is that by sharing what I've learned you can get a clearer picture now, far sooner than I did.

Chapter 18: The Landing

Five hundred twenty-five thousand six hundred minutes
How do you measure a life of a woman or a man?

—Jonathan Larson
From *Rent*

At the end of a show, when the curtain falls, do you feel like leaping to your feet, furiously clapping, and screaming with delight over what you just experienced? Are you so excited that you can't wait to tell your friends and family about the show and recommend everyone sees it?

Or do you sigh, shrug your shoulders, and look for the exit? You know then that while you may not bash the show, you're not going to recommend it. That's because everyone who worked on the show put their heart and skill into it, and you know how difficult that is, and you appreciate their commitment to the art.

Well, what if you're the show, and the audience? How do you want people to think and feel about you after your curtain drops? For what do you want to be known?

I'm still writing the end of my show, and I hope I still will be for many years to come.

But I'll tell you what, I want my family to know, beyond a shadow of a doubt, that I loved them unreservedly. I may not always have been the best at showing it, but I tried as best as I knew how. I'm proud of every one of them, I believe in them, and I'll be cheering them on for as long as I am able.

I want my friends to know how much they've enriched my life. I appreciate how they've tolerated my foot faults in tennis, my white-knuckled drives to Lakers games, the stories I've told during our poker and bridge games, and so much more. I want nothing more from them than to think of me as a "good friend."

I want my former colleagues to work hard to make their dreams come true. To be true to their hearts. To act in keeping with their integrity and values. To be ethical in their decision making. To treat others the way they want to be treated. To put their talent first in everything they do. And when someone leaves their employ or they themselves leave a company, to do it with dignity and grace.

In writing this book I also want my former colleagues from Abrams Artists Agency to know how much they mean to me and how important they were in constructing what we built. They were the people who contributed to making the agency so successful. I am privileged to have worked alongside them for so many years, and I wish them only the best in everything they do. There are too many to name; you all know who you are.

I want the artists I represented and supported to know that they are a gift to the world. Without them life would be without beauty and wonder and meaning. I want them to know that I appreciated them, and I never for a second took their talent for granted. It never felt like work to me to go any production they were in. It felt like a treat that I was lucky to have. I cherish them all.

Most importantly, I want everyone who wants to be an artist or an agent or wants to start a business to know that they have within them the ability to get it done. They need to surround themselves with good people who will support them and lift them up. They need to try as best they can to balance the competing interests in their lives — family, friends, and associates.

I say all of this because, at this point in my life, what I've written here is how I want to be known and remembered. It wasn't always this way. At different periods, I would have said different things. I wish I'd always been able to feel and say these things in the way that I have now. Like Pablo Casals, I'm making progress.

I don't say these things out of regret. I say them because I love to teach, and I care enough about you, dear reader, to ask you to do something for yourself. I'd like for you to honestly write down that for which you want to be known. Even if you're only 22 years old, think about how you want to be remembered when you're 92. What mark do you want to leave? When the curtain drops on your show, what do you want the audience to do? How do you want them to feel? If you're not happy with something in your life, work to change it. If you have something you want to do, work to make it happen.

Give this show everything you've got, and I guarantee you'll have them dancing in the aisles when you're through. Go get 'em!

Chapter 19: A Look Ahead

Anything can happen.

—Anthony Drewe, George Stiles
From *Mary Poppins*

The other day I went to the SoHo House in Los Angeles for lunch with a longtime friend. He's the CEO of a literary agency, and we'd dined together at that spot countless times over many years, in part, because my own agency was in that building before it moved to its current location.

When I walked into the lobby that day, I noticed that the name of my former company, Abrams Artists Agency, was still listed on the wall in the building directory. I smiled at the thought that I still had a presence in the building even if I wasn't there every day.

Moreover, meeting my old friend, in our familiar place, while I am nearing the end of this book, made me reflect again on the job of a CEO, the industry I love, and what that all might mean to anyone reading my words. I've had lunches like these with people at all stages of their careers, both in and out of the entertainment industry, and I've enjoyed dispensing wisdom and insights whenever I can.

I've already written about what it means to be a CEO, whether it's starting your own business, being promoted into the role, taking over another company, and even being the CEO of your own life. It's a roller-coaster ride of wins and losses, loyalties and betrayals, broken hearts and dreams come true – and I wouldn't trade it for any other job in the world.

When I think about one of the most important responsibilities of a CEO it is hard to accurately articulate it, but I want to give it a try. That's because what I'm about to say is at once impossible to achieve and essential to try – a CEO must see around corners. What I mean by that is this: CEOs need to be able to see what the future holds – good or bad – without getting their heads knocked off.

On the one hand, they need to be able to avoid dangers that could hurt or even kill their business.

On the other hand, they need to be able to take advantage of opportunities that could help them grow revenue, profit, and share – whatever their success metrics may be. In practice, this means staying connected to what's going on, constantly talking with people, watching trends, interpreting data, understanding new developments, getting perspectives from other industries and markets to see how they might apply to yours, and dipping your toe into a new venture before you dive all the way in.

One of the most valuable ways I've done that is by talking with my peers, other CEOs, like my friend. When we get together, we don't "do lunch" in the stereotypical insincere Hollywood way. We talk honestly and share information, use each other as sounding boards, and pick each other up when the other is down. We may commiserate about the dismal state of things from time to time, but we never leave it that way.

So let me share a bit about what I see coming around the corner. You can apply my thoughts to your own industry and situation in life. The entertainment industry is a complicated environment, comprised of business and creative components with a driving force and dependency on innovation and technology. The balance of profit and artistry is delicate and always evolving as well as who holds the power.

First, the speed of change in the entertainment industry is breathtaking. I don't know if it's faster or slower than in other industries, but I do know that technology is an accelerant that's disrupting many aspects of the business. That includes how businesses are structured, how work gets done, how businesses are started or dissolved or sold, how revenue and profits are derived, how people are compensated, how products are distributed and experienced, how marketing and publicity is done, and more.

This is especially true with the motion picture industry. Although some movies are still shot with film cameras, edited by cutting and splicing the old-fashioned way, distributed via ground and air transportation, and projected using film reels in big theaters, most movies now handle that entire workstream digitally. This means, among other things, that even before COVID-19 shut everything down, people could avoid having to go to a theater at a specific time and place, buy overpriced popcorn, and endure people talking and coughing right next to them because they could enjoy movies in the comfort of their homes. Where the studios once held all the power, it is now the consumer, enabled by the big streaming services who are not only distributing movies, but producing them; whether it is the same quality is left up to the viewer. Don't get me wrong, I love going to the movies with friends and family, reclining in a comfortable seat, munching on a snack, watching beautiful cinematography wash over a massive screen. But during the COVID-19 pandemic I have enjoyed not missing a beat because Amazon, Apple, Netflix, and all the other streaming services made it possible. I see this entire dynamic continuing and changing even further though I can't say how just yet.

Also, while people will always go to movie theaters to experience the latest superhero film on the big screen with their dates, it will happen less so. As a result, the studios who own those creative properties will have to be a lot more imaginative with their marketing and merchandising and partnerships if they want to make profits on their high-budget blockbusters. Likewise, movie theaters will have to find more creative ways to entice filmgoers to leave home and come to their theaters.

Another development is that competitors will come from anywhere. Who would have thought that Amazon, which began as an online bookseller, would be producing high quality movies and television? Or that a software company like Microsoft would buy an entertainment company like Activision for $70 billion? And Netflix – I know someone who was in a meeting at Harvard many years ago, with Reed Hastings, the founder of Netflix, who said, back in the days when they were renting out DVDs by mail, that they were going to beat Blockbuster and ultimately produce their own entertainment products – and Hastings was laughed at. Well, look at Netflix now. And today we've got a social media site, Facebook, changing its name to Meta and talking about something called the metaverse. What will go into that metaverse, which I imagine will include an untold amount of companies vying for mindshare and market share, I can't begin to tell you. What I can say is the metaverse will probably generate new opportunities and challenges the likes of which we can't even conceive.

Speaking of competition coming from everywhere, talent agencies are diversifying, creating their own content, and becoming more like media companies. They can't survive on 10 percent commissions anymore, especially since the Writers Guild of America won their recent battle with the agencies about packaging. Creating their own intellectual property enables the agencies to drive more revenue, so I don't see that stopping anytime soon.

After starting my career at MCA, going through the agency's expansion into production and distribution as they sought out new sources of revenue and influence, and experiencing MCA's forced breakup by U.S. Attorney General Robert F. Kennedy due to antitrust concerns, I did not think I'd see agencies expand into adjacent areas like MCA did. Time will tell whether the pendulum swings back again, and the government steps in and breaks them up.

As I am finishing this book, the Hollywood industry is at a crossroads. The WGA and SAG AFTRA are striking in unison. In a dramatic statement and one that I believe is accurate…George Clooney has called the strikes "an inflection point in our industry," and said that change is required for "our industry to survive." For example, how does the industry tackle the rise of Artificial Intelligence? True, they can make movies about it but what do you do when it comes for you. And how does one deal with the fact that while there are infinitely more opportunities for writers and actors, the majority of jobs no longer produce the same compensation they used to. You won't hear Mr. Clooney opine on either of these intractable questions. But someone will have to in order for the strike to be settled.

The last time both the Actors and the Writers went out on strike together was in 1960. After a very long and painful work stoppage the essential branches of Hollywood; the actors, the writers and producers negotiated a fair and equitable structure that has served the industry well. It may be painful and take way too long, but I believe at some point cooler heads will prevail and a new structure will emerge that takes the industry forward for another fifty years. There is too much at stake and too many skilled negotiators with nothing to do to keep an agreement from being reached.

In the commercial world, technology will continue to cause disruptive changes. Cord cutting, for example, which is when television viewers cancel their multichannel cable, satellite, and other pay TV subscription services, is accelerating. This has been going on for some time, but technology and broadcast innovations such as over-the-top media outlets and streaming services has sent the changes into overdrive.

For instance, the share of Americans who say they watch television via cable or satellite has plunged from 76 percent in 2015 to 56 percent in 2021, according to a new Pew Research Center survey of U.S. adults. Some 71 percent of those who do not use cable or satellite services say it's because they can access the content they want online, while 69 percent say the cost of cable and satellite services is too high and 45 percent say they do not often watch TV.

And this dynamic is picking up speed. More than 46 million U.S. households will have cut their pay TV cord by 2024. This phenomenon is especially popular among young audiences as viewers between the ages of 18 and 34 are most accustomed to non-linear entertainment formats and mobile streaming alternatives. But it doesn't stop there. Fewer than half of those ages 30 to 49 currently get TV that way, down 27 points. Among those 50 and older, the decline has been less dramatic: Those ages 50 to 64 saw a 14-point drop since 2015. Those 65 and older saw a 5-point decline, which is not a statistically significant difference.

This all has a huge impact on the commercial world as advertising continues to move to the internet. For brands, which rely on analytics to drive decisions, digital gets them in front of the eyes of specific demographics. That's terrific. For actors, there has been a big increase in non-union jobs which makes it much harder for actors starting out to use commercials as a decent source of revenue. Also, it is now much easier to create an ad using an iPhone and use non-union talent than ever before. When everyone can be a brand, producer, talent, talent representative, distributor, and consumer the whole industry is thrown into flux. It's happening now, and it will continue to happen.

What will never change in the entertainment industry is the need to create good stories, and the hunger to consume them. Much has been written about the role of storytelling our culture, so I won't belabor the point. I will say this: stories are how we make sense of the world, and therefore they will always have a place in our lives.

They've certainly had a place in mine, and for that I'll always be grateful to the people who create them.

Which brings me full circle. I began my working life selling stories on street corners – via newspapers – on the streets of Los Angeles, not too far from where I sat with my friend over lunch. And now I'm back on those streets, still looking around corners, still hungering for stories, and even telling some with this book.

I'll end the way I began my lunch. After my friend said to me, "It's good to see you, Harry," I said what I always do: "It's good to be seen."

It is indeed.

Acknowledgments

Thank you to Rod Thorn, my co-writer, who worked tirelessly, day in and day out, to co-write this book.

Thank you to Alan Morell, my literary agent, who advised and counseled me from the germ of an idea to the finished product.

Thank you to the publisher, John T. Colby Jr. of Brick Tower Press, for all of your support, insight, and guidance.

Thank you to my son Tony, my first-born child. Your memories and knowledge of earlier business years combined with your skills and insight as a screenwriter/director were an invaluable asset.

Thank you to the hundreds of agents, employees, actors, producers, directors, casting directors, co-workers, associates and friends who were interviewed and contributed to this book. I am eternally grateful for all of you. I am eternally grateful for all of you.

About Harry Abrams

Founder and former Chairman/Chief Executive Officer of Abrams Artists Agency, Harry Abrams, always knew that he wanted to pursue a career in the entertainment industry as a talent agent. After graduating with a B.S. in Business Administration from UCLA, in 1957, he worked in Indiana for a company that sold lawn mowers. In 1958, he joined MCA Artists, which was then a talent agency. Mr. Abrams started at an entry level position in the mailroom of MCA for forty dollars a week and rose quickly to become an administrative assistant in its television department. After working as an agent-in-training for 2 1/2 years, he was promoted to become an agent in the television department. He remained at MCA until 1962, when the company was forced to divest itself of its talent agency division due to an anti-trust action against MCA's parent company. The parent company for MCA also owned Universal Pictures/Studios and Revue Television Production Studios and would employ their own talent, to the dismay of rival talent agencies. The Attorney General of the United States at the time, Robert Kennedy, declared MCA a monopoly and forced them to choose between becoming either a production company or a talent agency. The parent company chose motion picture and television production. MCA Artists Agency was then disenfranchised by SAG along with the other unions. It was at this time that Mr. Abrams and an MCA co-worker decided to start their own specialized talent agency named Abrams-Rubaloff & Associates in Los Angeles.

The agency focused on representing broadcast journalists, radio and television personalities, newscasters, sportscasters, emcees/hosts for game and talk shows, radio and television performers for commercials, as well as spokesmen and spokeswomen on behalf of products. By 1966, the Los Angeles office was thriving, which allowed Mr. Abrams to move to the East coast and open a New York City branch of the agency. By 1977, Abrams-Rubaloff & Associates had risen to become the top talent agency of its kind throughout the country.

The rich theatrical environment of New York City captured Mr. Abrams' curiosity as he quickly became enamored with the theatrical actor. He discovered and guided a number of these performers, but only insofar as commercials were concerned. Mr. Abrams felt it would be beneficial to represent these performers for theatrical employment as well. Mr. Rubaloff did not share Mr. Abrams' ambitions. In 1977 they parted ways and Mr. Abrams went on to form in New York City what we now know as Abrams Artists Agency. This being an independent venture, he was able to create a talent agency that fit his own personal vision; a full-service agency (motion pictures, television, legitimate theater, radio and television commercials, etc.)

During the years from 1977 to 1982, Mr. Abrams would periodically make business trips to the Los Angeles area to present his New York clientele to motion picture and television producers on the West coast. He established affiliations with Los Angeles-based talent agencies to service the New York clientele. These reciprocal arrangements also allowed him to solicit employment in New York for the clients of the Los Angeles-based agencies. However, it was always his goal to have his own Los Angeles office rather than depend upon corresponding agency relationships. This goal was attained in 1982 with the opening of an agency known as Abrams, Harris & Goldberg in Los Angeles, a subsidiary of Abrams Artists & Associates in New York. Mr. Abrams traveled back and forth regularly between New York and Los Angeles, sometimes on a weekly basis, while he trained Mr. Harris and Mr. Goldberg in how to manage an agency and the fine points of how to run a business operation. During this time, Mr. Abrams continued to operate out of his New York office. It was not until 1986, when he separated from Mr. Harris and Mr. Goldberg, that he renamed the Los Angeles office, The Abrams Artists Agency, and moved back to Los Angeles to lead the West Coast office until retirement.

Mr. Abrams currently resides in Los Angeles with his wife, Gay. He also maintains a residence in New York City. Mr. Abrams has been on The Board of Directors of the Los Angeles Fraternity of Friends (a fundraising organization attached to The Music Center of Los Angeles), a major sponsor of the annual Sundance Film Festival, a supporter of the Theater Arts/Film School at UCLA, a member of the Independent Feature Film Project East/West, a member of the Los Angeles Entertainment Arts Council, a member of the Board of Directors of the Mark Taper Forum/Ahmanson/Kirk Douglas Theatre (The Center Theatre Group), a patron of the New York City Ballet and American Ballet Theater, a member of the East Hampton Tennis Club and the Riviera Tennis Club (Pacific Palisades, California). Mr. Abrams was also on the board of directors of REPRISE, a nonprofit theatre company that revived Broadway musicals for presentation several times a year at UCLA's Freud Theatre.

Now that Mr. Abrams is retired, he has the time to spend with his children and their growing families that are spread around the country.

Some recognizable performers for whom Mr. Abrams has been personally responsible and whose professional careers he has assisted in guiding are Liam Neeson, Sterling K. Brown, Michael B. Jordan, James Avery, Jaclyn Smith, Jennifer Lopez, Kerry Washington, Katie Holmes, David Strathairn, Connie Britton, Mason Adams, Bob Barker, Julia Barr, Susan Blakely, Ted Brown, Arte Johnson, Jim Lange, Susan Lucci, Wink Martindale, George Michaels, Chris Burke, Seymour Cassel, Lee J. Cobb, Bob Crane, Michael Emerson, Dick Enberg, Bob Eubanks, Andrea Evans, Mary Fickett, Matt Frewer, Lindsay Frost, Bob Gunton, Veronica Hamel, Chick Hearn, Dan Ingram, Judith Ivey, Brian Doyle Murray, Gary Owens, Regis Philbin, Avery Schreiber, Mal Sharpe, John Spencer, Ralph Story, Bill Stout, Senator Fred Dalton Thompson, Ruth Warrick, and Chandra Wilson.

For sales, editorial information, subsidiary rights information
or a catalog, please write or phone or e-mail
Brick Tower Press
Manhanset House
Shelter Island Hts., New York 11965, US
Tel: 212-427-7139
www.BrickTowerPress.com
bricktower@aol.com
www.IngramContent.com

For sales in the UK and Europe please contact our distributor,
Gazelle Book Services
White Cross Mills
Lancaster, LA1 4XS, UK
Tel: (01524) 68765 Fax: (01524) 63232
email: jacky@gazellebooks.co.uk

Printed in the USA
CPSIA information can be obtained
at www.ICGtesting.com
LVHW051827301023
762209LV00031B/608/J